# They Did Their Duty

## Oakwood Cemetery and the War of 1812

Cheryl E. Waterman

Published by
Turner Junction Publishing
West Chicago, Illinois

They Did Their Duty

War of 1812 Veterans buried in Oakwood Cemetery, West Chicago, IL with the stories of their service and lives.

First printing July, 2012.

ISBN13: 978-1475273137
ISBN10: 1475273134

Published by Turner Junction Publishing
West Chicago, Illinois USA.
Printed in the United States.

This book is dedicated to my number one encourager and love of my life, husband Ray, whose hand of support is always on my shoulder.

Any mistakes or incorrect conclusions are those of the author alone. Additional information is welcomed via e-mail at the following address:

*cherylewaterman@gmail.com*

# Table of Contents

# Declaration of War

## An Act Declaring War Between the United Kingdom of Great Britain and Ireland and the Dependencies Thereof and the United States of America and Their Territories.

*Be it enacted by the Senate and House of Representa–*
*tives of the United States of America in Congress*
*assembled,* That war be and the same is hereby declared to
exist between the United Kingdom of Great Britain and
Ireland and the dependencies thereof, and the United States
of America and their territories; and that the President of
the United States is hereby authorized to use the whole
land and naval force of the United States to carry the same
into effect, and to issue to private armed vessels of the
United States commissions or letters of marque and
general reprisal, in such form as he shall think proper, and
under the seal of the United States, against the vessels,
goods, and effects of the government of the said United
Kingdom of Great Britain and Ireland, and the subjects
thereof.

APPROVED, June 18, 1812[1]

---

[1]  1 May 2012. <www.thewarof1812.com/Warof1812documents/
declarationofwar.htm>

# Preface

A long time ago when I read a book about a monkey named Curious George, I thought my mother really should have named me Curious Georgia. I have a curiosity about people that transcends most people I know.

When we moved to West Chicago, Illinois, I became very curious about people buried by my house in Oakwood Cemetery. Then, while volunteering for a project at the West Chicago Museum, I became acquainted with some research done in previous years, and I wondered if we could now find more because of the advances of the Internet, online records and digitized books. I was especially interested in the War of 1812 veterans, four or five of whom were buried in West Chicago's oldest cemetery, Oakwood. Since West Chicago did not exist at the time of this war, I wondered how they came to be buried here. I was not interested in writing a rehash of the history of the War of 1812 but simply the story of the War, shown through events lived out in the men buried here.

Thus, I began my almost two year project of intense research. That war started two hundred years ago on June 18, 1812, and is often called "The Forgotten War," "President Madison's War," or "Jemmy's War." The war was officially finished in the spring of 1815. I started with five veterans from this war, but failed to prove any service for one.

Who were these men?

Where did they live in their lifetimes, and what brought them to be buried in Oakwood?

Could the way they lived their lives and their character teach us anything today? What lessons can we learn from them? With these goals in mind, I started researching everything I could find about them, good and bad.

In the 1960s Frank Scobey, now a deceased West Chicago Historian, wrote short biographies of each of these War of 1812 veterans in a local newspaper column. Today, with digitized records and greater facility in researching, we are able to find more records of their lives, and fill in some of the gaps.

These are the four proven War of 1812 veterans buried in Oakwood Cemetery, whose lives are detailed in following chapters:

**Daniel Benjamin**—one of the first settlers to Wayne Township, triumphing through murder, kidnapping, and pioneering throughout the Northwest Territory

**James Snyder**—an almost "accidental" member of the Turner community after pioneering in northern New York, western Illinois, and farming in Stephenson County for many years

**Daniel Wilson**—a member of a large, illustrious family who suffered much his entire life from one twenty-four hour period of war before joining other family members who migrated from New York to become early settlers in DuPage and Kane Counties, Illinois

**Daniel Wood**—a resident for most of his life in northern Vermont, next to the Canadian border, before leaving in his sixties to join other family members in Illinois

The fifth denizen of Oakwood reputed to be a veteran of that war is **John Haffey**. In his son-in-law Lucius B. Church's biographical sketch from a DuPage County history[2] Haffey is said to have served in the War. At this

---

[2] *Portrait and Biographical Record of Cook and DuPage Counties, Illinois: Containing Biographical Sketches of Prominent and Representative Citizens of the County, Together with Biographies*

point no proof of that service, or even of his life history before 1830 can be definitively discovered.

Most records record his birth at or near 1800, which means he was a little young to have served actively in the war. However, many officers had boys of that age serving as "Waiters" and some of their service went unrecorded. Perhaps at some future point more will be known about Haffey's life and his service in the war.

*and Portraits of All the Presidents of the United States* (Chicago: Lake City Pub. Co., 1894, Internet Resource), 164.

They Did Their Duty

# 1.
# Oakwood Cemetery and the Village of Turner

When Oakwood Cemetery was founded in 1858, there was no village of West Chicago. The city's website says the following about the founding of West Chicago:

> John B. Turner, president of the G&CU and a resident of Chicago, owned several acres of land in what is now the center of town. As more people settled in Junction, Turner recognized the chance to make a profit by platting his land and selling off lots. He therefore recorded the community's first plat in 1855 under the name of Town of Junction.
>
> The community continued its growth, and in 1857 Dr. Joseph McConnell and his wife Mary platted a second portion of town just north of John B. Turner's plat. They recorded their plat as the Town of Turner in honor of the railroad president. These two "towns" became informally known as Turner Junction.[3]

---

[3]    18 Jun. 2012 <www.westchicago.org/Community/ Early History.html>.

By 1873 there were enough inhabitants that the area was officially incorporated as the Village of Turner, and Lucius B. Church was the first village president.

Back in September of 1858, Jonathan Valette, surveyor, certified in court that according to orders from the directors and officers of the proposed Oakwood Cemetery, he had surveyed and laid out 198 plots along with ten foot wide alleys for horse and buggy carriages on land formerly part of the J. McConnell farm. Great detail was given regarding the numbering of the plots and their sizes. Most were either 8 or 9 feet wide, and 19 to 24 feet in length.

In addition, stones, many still existing today, were set into the corners of each lot. Approximately 22 lots were set aside and suggested to be used for strangers and indigent persons.

In December of 1858, formation papers were certified and signed in the County Court of DuPage by the Officers and Directors for Oakwood Cemetery. J.M. McConnell, owner of the land, was the President. J.A. Smith was both Treasurer and Secretary, and James Conolly, Charles Winslow and Daniel Wood were the Directors.[4]

Later, in 1869 a cemetery act was passed by the State Congress to enable the Directors to assess each lot a fee, not exceeding one dollar per year.[5] Even so, at various times throughout the years the cemetery would fall into disrepair.

Until the 1890s, cattle would graze through a side gate. At some point the outside iron fence, gates, and arched main entrance disappeared. Tombstones aged, some cracked, and some were defaced by vandals or even taken.

---

[4] This information was found in copies of papers that accompanied the original cemetery plat, in the West Chicago Museum files.

[5] *Private Laws of the State of Illinois: Passed by the Twenty-Sixth General Assembly, Convened January 4, 1869* (Springfield: Illinois Journal Printing Off, 1869, Internet resource), 327.

Worst of all, all the original sales of lots, burial records, and even the original maps disappeared. Finally, in 1965, the cemetery was turned over to the village of West Chicago to administer and use.

By the 1890s the village wanted to attract industry, and be more than just a village. Since they were west of Chicago, and since Chicago had a lot of industry, in 1896 the Village of Turner became West Chicago.

.

# 2.
# Daniel Benjamin

## "Push Forward"

Daniel Benjamin, one of the earliest settlers to Wayne Township in DuPage County, was the first of the War of 1812 veterans buried in Oakwood Cemetery to serve in that war. War had been part of his life from an early age. Family members had already served in various French and Indian Wars, and Jonathan, his father's brother, said he had gone to war the first time when he was but fourteen years of age.[6]

### THE BENJAMIN HERITAGE

Born between 1766 and 1772, probably in Orange County, New York, Daniel was the sixth generation of his family in the New World, with his ancestor, John Benjamin, having arrived in the Boston Harbor from England in 1632.[7] Several genealogies have been written on the Benjamin family, and it is interesting to note that they claim a family motto, "Poussez en avant" or "Push

---

[6]  Samuel Park, *Notes of the Early History of Union Township, Licking County, Ohio* (Terre Haute, IN: O.J. Smith & Co., 1870, Internet resource), 20.

[7]  Gloria W. Bicha and Helen B. Brown, *The Benjamin Family in America* (Racine: Bicha, 1977, Internet resource), 6.

Forward." [8] These two words could summarize Daniel Benjamin's life.

In about 1773-4, his family moved from the Goshen, New York area to land by the Loyalsock Creek, then in Northumberland County, Pennsylvania, along the Susquehanna River. Northumberland had been made available for purchase in 1772.[9] They were looking for a place to settle where they would have land to farm, and moved there even though there were still some problems with natives.

Daniel's mother, Elizabeth, was the daughter of Daniel Brown, and she and her sister, Margaret, married the Benjamin brothers, David and Jonathan.[10] Both families, along with the grandparents and a collection of other family members made this move to become early settlers in this part of Pennsylvania,[11]

*Moving together as community and family as well as being caring citizens, actively concerned in community government were patterns in his life.*

Somewhere between May of 1775 and December, 1778, but most likely some time in 1777,[12] their Loyalsock settlement was attacked by Indians. Various accounts have been written, and trying to find the exact truth is difficult.

---

[8] Ellis Benjamin Baker, *Genealogy of the Benjamin Family in the United States of America from 1632 to 1898: Containing the Families of John 1, Joseph 2, Joseph 3, Joseph 4, Joseph 5, and Judah 6 and the Descendants of Orange Benjamin 7 of Mount Washington, Mass.* (New Haven, Conn: Press of Tuttle, Morehouse & Taylor, 1898, Internet resource), 9.

[9] "Newsblog: This Is the News," *Timeline*, 15 May 2012 <http://www.newsofyesteryear.com/resources/timeline>

[10] John F. Meginness, *History of Lycoming County, Pennsylvania* (Chicago: Brown, Runk, 1892, Internet resource), Chapter VI.

[11] Bicha 705.

[12] Meginness, Chapter VI. Park's book puts the date at 1775 (p 20).

Some descendants say the attack must have taken place in the spring of 1778 because names of the captured/killed men were still on the tax lists of 1778. However, in the Revolutionary War Pension file of Daniel's uncle, Jonathan Benjamin points to the possible Indian skirmish being some time in 1777. He served for six months from January, 1776, in Captain Joseph Newman's Company; immediately after he then served nine months from June or July, 1776, in Captain Hepburn's Company. He then stayed home about one year, and commenced serving again in Captain Hepburn's Company another three years.[13] Timewise this agrees perfectly with an account by J. F. Meginness.

To our knowledge, no account of his captivity was written by Daniel himself, though descendants and other historians have written of it. In addition, many historians have drawn from parts of two main accounts which are found in their entirety at the end of this chapter.

Samuel Park, born in 1804, personally knew Daniel's mother, brother David, and Uncle Jonathan, along with other family members living in Licking County, Ohio. He appears to be the earliest to write and publish in 1870 the version of the attack as he knew it.[14]

In summary, as the Indians attacked, it appears that Daniel's father, David Benjamin, Daniel's maternal grandparents, and an aunt were killed. David was scalped to death in front of the family and the Browns and the aunt were burned alive in their cabin.

Daniel and five siblings, David, Nathan, Ezekiel, William, an unnamed sister, and his mother were carried

---

[13] Pension file S31811, Snyder, Jonathan, Revolutionary War, *Fold3.com*, Series: M804, Pennsylvania> B> Benjamin> Jonathan Benjamin, accessed 16 Feb 2012.

[14] Park, see Appendix B.

into captivity along with about four others: "In the fall of 1777, three families totaling 16 members were attacked along Loyalsock Creek; four were killed and the remainder carried into captivity."[15] While in captivity, they probably were split up and divided amongst different tribes.

Daniel's Uncle Jonathan and his family escaped being taken because of living on the opposite side of Loyalsock Creek, though their cabins were burned as the Indians shot flaming arrows at them. Park remembers him in this way:

> Jonathan Benjamin was in some respects an extraordinary man. He was a person of rather coarse features, but of strong muscular powers, with a still stronger will. He was very determined in all of his undertakings, and of rather an unforgiving temperament. Having passed through the French and Indian wars, and through the war of the Revolution, and having suffered much and long by Indian depredations, both in the loss of friends and property, the finer feelings of his nature had become blunted to such an extent that he seemed to have lost most of his sympathy for his fellow man. Still he was a man of religious habits, and of good morals, but was generally considered to be a man that was naturally morose and unsociable, and I believe was not known through life to have expressed his forgiveness of the Indian race.[16]

Ezekiel Brown, brother of Elizabeth and Margaret Benjamin and uncle to Daniel, was also one of those captured that day. At some point he managed to obtain freedom and then devoted his life to searching for his family, freeing them one by one.[17]   In the years that

---

[15] James R. Williamson and Linda A. Fossler, *The Susquehanna Frontier: Northeastern Pennsylvania During the Revolutionary Years* (Wilkes-Barre, PA: Wilkes University Press, 1997), 29.
[16] Park 19-20.

They Did Their Duty

followed their release, William Benjamin, probably the eldest brother, became guardian of the youngest sibling (name unknown), and became owner of the land his father had tried to settle. William remained in Pennsylvania until his death in 1830.[18]

Their captured sister was returned and tried living with white civilization again for a time, but could not adjust. She had been married to an Indian and had borne him children. After some time, she returned to her Indian family and was lost to the Benjamins.

Twenty-five years after Samuel Park's account, John Franklin Meginness wrote several books of Pennsylvania history, including his findings of the tragedy in his *History of Lycoming County, Pennsylvania* in 1895.[19] Lycoming County had been formed from Northumberland County in 1795[20], and the Loyalsock settlement was in the new county.

Daniel is said to have been five years old when captured and thirteen when released.[21] If the attack was in 1777, then the 1772 birth date found on the 1850 census record would be more correct than the 1766 record on his tombstone. The captives were said to have been released around 1884[22], which would also fit with the later birth date. Whatever the details, the aftereffects of those years with the Indians resonated through the following generations.

## THE FAMILY MOVES ON WITH LIFE

When the Benjamin family was freed, they remained in

---

[17] Meginness, Chapter VI.
[18] Bicha 745.
[19] See Appendix B
[20] Meginness, Chapter V.
[21] Scobey's Notes at the West Chicago Museum
[22] Bicha 742.

Pennsylvania for some years. As the first United States Federal census was enumerated in 1790, as proscribed by the new Constitution, the Lycoming area of the Northumberland, Pennsylvania census showed "Widow Benjamin" with five others. "Jonathan Benjamin," whose wife was the widow's sister, was listed one name later. Her brothers Ezekiel and Daniel Brown and families are in the second column.[23]

According to Bicha's notes[24], a Daniel Benjamin owned 400 acres in Huntingdon County, Pennsylvania, in 1793. This may or may not be our Daniel.

David, Nathan (Nathaniel),[25] Ezekiel[26] and Daniel all "Pushed Forward" later settling in various parts of Ohio before Daniel moved even farther west.

At that time the territory west of the Appalachian Mountains was not officially open to settlers, and was reserved for the Indians. Lands presently containing the entire states of Ohio, Indiana, Illinois, Michigan, Wisconsin, and part of Minnesota were ceded to the United States in the Treaty of Paris in 1783. With the signing of the Ordinance of the Northwest Territory on July 14, 1787, settlers were given rights to own the land and to pass it to their heirs along with guidelines of how the land would be governed. The first permanent 48 settlers arrived in Marietta (Ohio) in 1788[27].

Daniel married Martha Young, daughter of Robert Young, either in Pennsylvania or in Ohio. With Robert

---

[23]  1790 US census, Northumberland, Pennsylvania; Series: M637; Roll: 9; Page: 42; Image: 279; Family History Library Film: 0568149. Accessed ancestry.com 12 Dec 2011.
[24]  Bicha 744.
[25]  Jackson, Ronald V., Accelerated Indexing Systems, comp.. *Ohio Census, 1790-1890* [database on-line]. Provo, UT, USA: Ancestry.com Operations Inc, 1999. Accessed 01 Dec 2011.
[26]  *Ibid.*
[27]  20 May 2012 <http://www.mariettaohio.info/history/pioneers/>

Young being a common name, it is not possible at this time to determine which one was her father, though Derry Township of Northumberland County contained the family of a Robert Young who looks likely.

At some point in the late 1790's, many of the Benjamin family community moved west into the Marietta area. The Treaty of Grenville had been signed on August 3, 1795, putting an end to an Indian war, with General Anthony Wayne (of "Fort Wayne, Indiana" fame) representing the American side. The Indians relinquished claim to most of Ohio and the Detroit and Chicago areas. With the signing of this treaty, settlers began to pour into Ohio.

Brother David along with another brother (Daniel or Nathan?) moved from the Susquehanna to the Marietta area in 1795.[28] By the early 1800s the families had moved a little farther west and north, some settling by Auter Creek in what is presently Licking County, Ohio, and others, including Daniel, near present day Columbus, on the banks of the Scioto River[29.] An eyewitness described them thusly: "The settlers lent each other aid in their raisings and other heavy operations requiring many hands. By thus mutually assisting one another, they were all enabled, in due season, to provide themselves with cabins to live in, and prepare their clearings for farming."[30]

*Family was important to them, and they looked out for each other.*

In 1803 Ohio became a state. On February 4, 1805, Daniel received a $2 bounty for pelts of wolves and panthers. His family was growing, and in 1808 his son

---

[28] Park 33.
[29] Jackson, Ronald V., Accelerated Indexing Systems, comp.. *Ohio Census, 1790-1890* [database on-line]. Provo, UT, USA: Ancestry.com Operations Inc, 1999. Accessed 01 Dec 2011.
[30] Sanderson 16-17.

Robert Young Benjamin was born. There is a persistent undocumented tradition that he was the eldest son and the third child. Though no complete proof has been found, Margaret is said to have been the first daughter, born about 1803.[31] Elizabeth, the second daughter, was born about 1806.

From 1805 to 1810 Daniel was mustered in some sort of community militia in Franklin County. On February 3, 1810, he is recorded as pledging $50 as a citizen of Worthington, Ohio, towards building a state house.[32] Unfortunately, the 1800 and 1810 federal census records have been lost for that area, so no records are available to help us know more about his family.

The fledgling country of the United States was still struggling as it attempted to establish its own identity. England may have signed a treaty giving independence to the colonies, but in reality they were still acting in many ways as if the colonies were still their property.

Not only were they struggling with the British, but the Americans were also having varying success in their relationships with the Indians. The Americans wanted more land, but the Indians considered it to be their land.

William Henry Harrison was a military man who wanted to secure legal titles to the land for the United States and negotiated treaties with the Indians. The biggest was the Treaty of Fort Wayne on Sept 30, 1809, which sold 3,000,000 acres to the United States. President James Madison supported this treaty which opened much of Indiana to new settlement.

---

[31] Ancestry.com. Yates Publishing. *U.S. and International Marriage Records, 1560-1900* [database on-line]. Provo, UT, USA: Ancestry.com Operations Inc, 2004. Source number: *1671.047*.
[32] Bicha 744.

However, in Indiana, near the present-day city of Lafayette, a confederacy of Indians opposed United States expansion. Their chief, Tecumseh, and his brother Tenskwatawa, called the Prophet, called for a return to ancestral ways, and wanted them to nullify the treaties.

In November, 1811, Harrison had arranged to meet with Tenskwatawa near the Tippecanoe River and their village Prophetstown. While waiting, the warriors attacked him. After hard fighting, the American military triumphed, burning the village and proclaiming victory. From this battle, Harrison then gained the nickname "Tippecanoe."

Later, in the Presidential campaign of 1840 the phrase "Tippecanoe and Tyler too" ("Tyler" referring to the Vice-Presidential candidate) became their election slogan. Harrison's detractors said that the battle was not much of a victory since the Indians soon rebuilt their town and frontier violence actually increased. Many natives of the Northwest Territory joined the British side during the War of 1812.

On April 29, 1812, as tensions were increasing, Governor Return Jonathan Meigs of Ohio gave orders to the military commanders of the area to bring their men to a meeting in Dayton. On May 25th, Governor William Hull of Michigan arrived in Dayton to assume command of the men.

After meetings with Indian chiefs to obtain permission

to take troops through their lands, the troops started northward toward the border with Canada, building roads and bridges along the way making it possible for them to continue. War was officially declared by the U.S. Congress against Great Britain on June 18. However, from all the muster rolls and research, it appears that Daniel Benjamin was not a part of this first campaign.

As the troops marched in the summer of 1812 towards Detroit to conquer it from the British, all was not well. Chicago had already been lost to the British. Then General William Hull, with orders to take Detroit, refused to let his men fire on the British, and instead raised a white flag of capitulation on August 16. His men had begun to question his abilities to lead and even his fidelity to the cause. With his angry regular army troops imprisoned, the Ohio militia men were taken to Cleveland and freed on parole after agreeing they would not fight again against the British. Most of those militia men did not keep that agreement.[33] General Hull along with his officers and imprisoned men were eventually taken by the British to Montreal where terms for their release were negotiated.

Later, the United States government court-martialed and convicted General Hull for cowardice, neglect of duty and unofficer-like conduct, sentencing him to be shot dead, but he was later pardoned by President Madison.[34] In retrospect, years later some historians said they thought the biggest defect of all the old veterans who also served in this war was the dementia of old age, a weakness instead of cowardice.[35]

---

[33] Benson J. Lossing, *Pictorial Field-Book of the War of 1812* (New York: Harper & Brothers, Pub., 1868, Internet Resource), 291.
[34] *Ibid.* 294.
[35] *Ibid.* 295.

As news of the humiliation of the United States troops in Detroit reached Daniel's area of Ohio, one can imagine this spurring him to enlist that first time on the 23rd of August:

> But these disasters, instead of depressing them, gave them increased elasticity and strength. The whole total of society bordering upon the Ohio River heaved, like a storm-smitten ocean in its wrath, with patriotic emotions.... Christian civilization, national pride, and an enlightened patriotism, all pleaded for vindication, and nobly was that plea responded to. When a call for troops was made, men of every class and condition of life—farmers, merchants, lawyers, physicians, and young men innumerable—flocked to the recruiting stations and offered their services.[36]

In 1812 Daniel Benjamin was between 40 and 46 years of age. Company muster roll cards and pay roll cards have been found for two short enlistments.

The first card for Daniel is from the 23rd of August to the 24th of September in 1812 as Private in Lieutenant Roswell Tuller's Ohio Militia, and the second from the 7th of October to the 17th of November, again in 1812, serving in Captain Aaron Strong's Company of Ohio Volunteers raised from Root's 3 Reg't Ohio Militia.

*No matter what their age, Benjamins served and continued to "Push Forward" as long as physically possible.*

With Chicago and Detroit under British control, much pressure was now on Fort Wayne, so some troops were sent there. Others were sent to guard the Indiana and

---

[36] *Ibid.* 321.

Illinois border area, especially at Vincennes and Terre Haute. By late November of 1812, though, Daniel was discharged from his short second enlistment, and probably returned home to help his family for the winter.

The American troops wanted to recapture Detroit, but had to deal with a lack of provisions, a lack of roads, and a mixture of militia from various states as well as a few "regular" United States military. The Ohio volunteers were put to work moving provisions from near the head of the Great Miami River, about twenty miles north of present-day Urbana up to Fort McArthur and Fort Findlay.[37]

Daniel Benjamin never applied for any benefits for his war service—neither bounty land nor pension. There was also no widow's pension. Therefore, we must look at records of people who served with him to gain an idea of exactly what he might personally have been doing.

The Lieutenant over Captain Strong's Company in the fall of 1812 was Chauncey Barker. As he applied for bounty land he explained how many times the militia served without accurate documentation. Whenever there was an alarm of any possible danger, the captains would collect their companies. Sometimes by the time everyone was ready the alarm would cease and they would go back

---

[37] Lossing 340.

to work. Their Regiment was considered a frontier regiment, bordering on the Indian boundary and alarms of many kinds were frequent.

In his second tour of 1812 Barker volunteered as a private under a call of Governor Meigs for a six months term and was elected Lieutenant, with Aaron Strong as Captain. They were employed in making roads and blockhouses toward Sandusky.

As they moved the provisions nearer to Sandusky and Lake Erie, they wanted to take advantage of hard ice on the rivers, allowing them to move with greater ease. However, the winter of later 1812 to spring of 1813 was extremely warm, and there was little or no ice, making it impossible to proceed with any speed. General Harrison therefore fortified his position at his camp near present Toledo, and waited for spring.[38] At the same time, knowing that British General Proctor, aided by Chief Tecumtha (sometimes written Tecumseh), wanted to take more of the Ohio territory, General Harrison needed new troops.[39] The one year terms of many of the first enlistees were expiring. So a new call for enlistments went out.

In 1851, long after the end of the war, George Sanderson, Esq., published a lecture on the early history of Fairfield County, Ohio in installments in the local Lancaster newspaper. It was subsequently published and is now available for all, having been digitized by Google. In Sanderson's lecture, he wrote of the kind of people those early settlers of the Scioto valley were. "The early settlers were a hardy and industrious people, and for frankness and hospitality have not been surpassed by any community. The men labored upon their farms and the women in their cabins."[40] He also gave descriptions of the food they ate

---

[38] *Ibid.* 473.
[39] *Ibid.* 475.
[40] George Sanderson, *A Brief History of the Early Settlement of*

and detailed the construction of their cabins, furniture, and everyday life. This was valuable eye witness writing and research done by a contemporary of Daniel Benjamin. In fact, George Sanderson was his Captain for a third enlistment.

As Harrison's call for enlistments went out, Daniel enlisted officially a third time on April 27, 1813, as a private in Capt. George Sanderson's newly organized Company. Though no muster or pay roll cards have been located for this service, Sanderson lists Daniel Benjamin as one of his privates in his 1851 booklet.[41]

Sanderson commanded two companies at two times during the war with Great Britain. The first was a company raised of volunteers for one year as part of the Ohio Volunteers commanded by Col. Lewis Cass. They were all captured at Fort Detroit on the 16th of August, 1812, and were part of those forced home on parole with the agreement of no more war service. Sanderson, himself one of the captives, was so exasperated with the unfortunate occurrences at Detroit and the behavior of General Hull that he joined General William Harrison, who later became President, and raised a second company.[42]

This new company was also recruited for a term of one full year in the spring of 1813 from Franklin, Fairfield, and Delaware Counties, and it is thought that they joined Harrison—"…speedily joined by four hundred and fifty more troops under Lieutenant Colonel George Paul, of the infantry."[43]  Harrison quickly arranged all the volunteers into eleven regiments, one of them being that of Lieutenant Colonel Paul.[44] Captain George Sanderson's Company was

---

*Fairfield County* (Lancaster, OH: Thomas Wetzler, 1851, Internet resource), 16-18.
[41]  *Ibid.* 32.
[42]  *Ibid.* 30-31.
[43]  Lossing 498.

part of this 27th Regiment commanded by Lt. Col. Paul, of Belmont County.[45]

Meanwhile, the navy was busy on Lake Erie, and in the summer of 1813, Commodore Perry gained a huge victory over the British. That made it possible for Harrison to retake Detroit, and pursue the British into Canada, up the Thames River towards Moravia Town. This is where they made their final stand, ending in American victory on the 5th of October, 1813. 120 regulars of the 27th Regiment were with him in this battle.[46] We don't know if Daniel was a part of this group or if he was part of the group left in Detroit to help the people to regain order after the mayhem of the battles. Harrison had made General Cass military and civil governor of Michigan and had ordered him to keep control of the Indians and hold that portion of the country.[47] General Harrison then left military service in the spring of 1814.[48]

The men of Sanderson's Company were honorably discharged from Fort Shelby (Detroit) in the spring and summer of 1814.[49] No doubt Daniel was glad to be home again in that summer as his wife had given birth to daughter Eunice on July 13, 1813, probably while he was

---

[44] *Ibid.* 545.
[45] Sanderson 31.
[46] Lossing 551.
[47] *Ibid.* 559.
[48] *Ibid.* 562.
[49] Sanderson 31.

away. Andrew probably was born next, and John followed on June 18, 1816. By that time the end of the war had come with the signing of the Treaty of Ghent on December 24, 1814, but not formally ratified by all until February 1815.

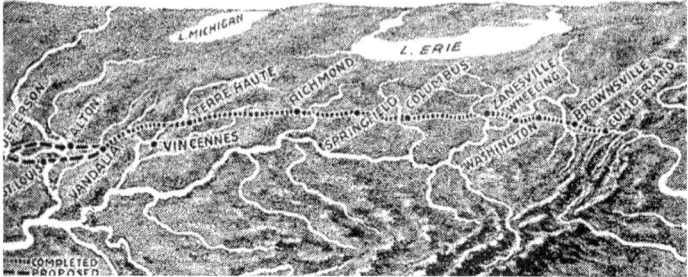

## THE FAMILY AGAIN MOVES WESTWARD

In 1816 the Indiana territory became a state with Illinois not far behind in 1818. Daniel and family pushed forward again, moving at some point between 1816 and 1820 to Vigo County, along the border between Indiana and Illinois. Terre Haute was an important outpost during the War of 1812 and though it is unknown whether or not Daniel may have been in this area under one of his enlistments, he would surely have heard of the area. The National Road, also known as the Cumberland Road, surveyed about 1806 and built between 1811 and 1837 went to Terre Haute directly west from Columbus, though it was not yet officially finished that far when the Benjamins arrived there. Daniel Benjamin was listed as head of a household of eleven in Vigo County in the 1820 US Census.

Even while Daniel and Martha were still occupied with their young children, the older ones were now marrying: Margaret married Luke Hankins (sometimes Hawkins) of Kentucky in 1822.[50] Robert married Nancy Grove (Groff,

Groves) of Hopkins County, Kentucky in February 25, 1826.[50] Elizabeth married George Billings, son of Increase and Rachel Billings in Fountain, Indiana on September 20, 1827.[52] The Billings had come to Indiana from Luzerne County, Pennsylvania.

Daniel was not satisfied to stay around Terre Haute, because he next moved north to the area that became Warren County, Indiana. In 1827 we find his name on the roll of those helping form the county.[53] In the 1830 federal census, he is present there, next to son Robert, and on the same page with the Billings. The Hankins are nearby on another page.

Meanwhile, back in Licking County, Ohio, Daniel Benjamin's mother, older brother David, and other family members had settled and stayed. In Samuel Park's book written in 1870 he reflects on the life of this brother David:

> David Benjamin was a frontiersman all his life, and so much of his youth having been spent among savages, he grew up without education, or much knowledge of the refinements of fashionable society, but he was a peaceable and a kindhearted citizen. He was cheerful, quite sociable, and very industrious. Although he often said he never could forgive the Indian race for the wrongs that he had suffered, still when a friendly Indian called at his door for bread, he never

---

[50] Ancestry.com. Source number: *1671.047*.

[51] "Indiana, Marriages, 1811-1959," index, FamilySearch (https://familysearch.org/pal:/MM9.1.1/JCJB-L7J : accessed 25 June 2012), George Billings, 1827.

[52] Dodd, Jordan, Liahona Research, comp.. *Indiana Marriages, 1802-1892* [database on-line]. Provo, UT, USA: Ancestry.com Operations Inc, 2004. Accessed 23 Jun 2012.

[53] *Counties of Warren, Benton, Jasper and Newton, Indiana: Historical and Biographical* (Chicago: F.A. Battey & Co, 1883, Internet resource), 59.

would turn him away till he supplied his wants. But when this was done, he would at once request him to leave. He seemed to fear that the remembrance of his wrongs would overcome his feelings of humanity, hence he would not suffer them to remain where they would be likely to tempt him, or excite his feelings of revenge."[54]

In the spring of 1834 David Benjamin died. His mother actually lived until the next year, spending many years without her husband and with some children near and others far away. Since David grew up "without education" one wonders if this was also true of Daniel. One also might wonder if communication was such that Daniel Benjamin and his family ever knew when his brother and mother died. Both brothers seemed to have the ability to deal calmly with Indians. We have evidence of this in Illinois through actions of Daniel's son, Robert Young Benjamin.[55]

By the early 1830's, the urge to "Push Forward" became strong again, and we find Daniel Benjamin moving again in community with several other families from Warren, Indiana to Cook County (present-day DuPage County), west of Chicago:

> Daniel Benjamin, the father, with his four sons - Andrew, John, Joseph and Robert Y.-and about ten other families, all came to the place together with their own teams, from Ohio, arriving at what is now Wayne on the 12th of May, 1834. All these families, except the Benjamins and Joseph Vale, whose family was one of the party, settled on the Fox River.[56]

The Vale family was also part of the Warren County

---

[54] Park 23, 24.
[55] Rufus Blanchard, *History of Du Page County, Illinois* (Chicago: O.L. Baskin & Co, 1882, Internet resource), 200.
[56] *Ibid.* 271.

group. Father John, born in England about 1780, had married Susannah Wolgamott, and they were the parents of Cynthia, Joseph, and Hester ("Susan"). Cynthia married Daniel's son Andrew at some point, either in Indiana or in Illinois. No record has been located to this point for that marriage. The Benjamins and Vales lived in the same area from Ohio to Indiana to Illinois, and later in Iowa.

Family lore says that Robert Benjamin made the trip from Illinois back to Warren, Indiana in 1835 to get his mother, Daniel's wife, who had remained there until they could build the cabins.

Illinois was to be the final settling place for Daniel and Martha, with many family members and friends nearby. Some of their children would continue to push west, with Andrew, Joseph and Margaret and others settling in Shelby and Van Buren Counties, Iowa. Robert and John stayed near them their whole lives, and the next generation spread through many more states. When the Civil War years arrived, some of his grandchildren carried on the long-time family tradition of serving their country in time of war.

> *Doing their duty to the utmost in serving their country was carried on through the generations.*

There is no record of any bounty land request from Daniel Benjamin, though he was entitled to receive it. Neither was there any request for a pension. He lived his final days on his farm and both Daniel and Martha died in January of 1863, only 11 days apart.

One family history gives a "Prayer of the Benjamin Family" said to be used in the 1800s[57]. In reviewing his life and the strength of character needed to overcome the obstacles, this prayer seems especially appropriate for Daniel:

---

[57] Bicha ii.

*Forsake me not, God, until I have shown my strength to this generation and to all that are to come.*

# 3.
# James Snyder

## "Ready at all times to go at call"

The second member of Oakwood Cemetery to serve in the war was an almost "accidental" member of the Turner community. He did not arrive in Turner until his old age, after pioneering in northern New York State, La Porte, Indiana, and western Illinois. Though he reportedly sired 14 children, we believe none were present at his death, and his written history has been distorted by some descendants.

According to his own testimony, James Snyder was born either in German Flats or Warren, Herkimer County, New York, in 1788.[58] This was part of the Mohawk Valley Region of New York. Herkimer County was not formed until 1791, and a little later part of this was taken to form Oneida and Onondaga Counties. Just as we say today that Snyder is buried in West Chicago, Illinois, when in his time it was actually Turner, Illinois, so in the 1800s he stated that he was born in Herkimer County when in actuality it was then still part of Montgomery County.

### THE SNYDER HERITAGE

Some family members say his father was a Christopher

---

[58] Pension file 21988, Snyder, James, War of 1812, National Archives, Washington, D.C., 10 Jan 2011.

Snyder of Holland, born about 1750. Though the descendants probably were thinking of Holland, the country, in reality the area where James was born was part of or near the Holland Land Patent given by the King of England to Lord Holland, and has nothing at all to do with Holland the country. The Snyder/Snider/Schneider family is well known in the Montgomery County area as part of the 1710 Palatinate migration from present day southern Germany. Our James Snyder probably comes either from this group or from the earlier group of settlers farther east who came from the Netherlands.

There are at least four Christopher Snyder/Snider families listed in the 1790 census, just after James is said to have been born, but none in the Warren, German Flats area. In the 1800 census there is a Jacob Snider listed in German Flats and a John Snider in Warren, but neither of them have a "male 10-16" which would have reflected his age at that time (12 years).[59]   Only the heads of the households are listed in the federal censuses until 1850.

## MARRIAGE AND MOVING NORTHWARD

The next date where we can positively locate James Snyder is on March 10, 1811, when, according to his own testimony, he marries Clara/ Clarissa/ Clarhacy Downer in Rome, Oneida County, New York.[60] Her Downer family had been in America for seven generations, from the mid-1600s, and Clarissa's father Stephen had moved his family from Connecticut to New York. Clarissa's siblings all finished life in various parts of Michigan. One Downer relative, Avery Downer, had moved north at this time to live in Ellisburg, Jefferson County, New York, about 43 miles north of Rome.

---

[59]  All census files accessed through Ancestry.com.
[60]  Pension file 21988.

Jefferson County was part of Oneida County until 1805 when it was split off and formed into its own county.[61] It was named for the then current president of the country, Thomas Jefferson, and Watertown was the county seat.

After the Revolutionary War, New York State made land available for purchase in Jefferson County. Two Ellis brothers had bought huge tracts, and in 1803, before the county was even officially formed in 1805, they founded the town of Ellisburgh. Most of today's maps have it as Ellisburg, without the "h." Traveling north from Rome was difficult until 1808 when a new road was constructed from Rome to Brownville, just north of Ellisburg.[62] This made it much easier for new settlers to arrive, and shortly after the Snyders married, they moved north to this area.

Nearby was Boyleston, just over the border today into what is now Oswego County. A history of that area tells of some of the early settlers:

> In Boyleston: Jacob, Reuben, Henry, Abram, and Jonathan Snyder, nearly all of whom were substantial farmers from the famous Mohawk Valley. Abram Snyder located on the homestead now occupied by where Ira Cummins now lives. The locality took from them the name of Snyder's Corners.[63]

By the 1820 United States Federal Census Christopher Snyder, a male over 45 years of age, along with a female over 45, is living in Watertown, the county seat of

---

[61]  20 Jun 2012 <http://jefferson.nygenweb.net/jeffhist.htm>

[62]  Jere Coughlin, Secretary, *Jefferson County Centennial* (Hungerford-Halbrook Co, Watertown, N. Y., 1905, Internet resource) Accessed 10 Feb 2012 <http://history.rays-place.com/ny/jeff-commerce.htm>

[63]  John C. Churchill, assisted by H. Perry Smith and W. Stanley Child, "History of Boylston, NY", *Landmarks of Oswego County* (Syracuse, NY: D. Mason & Co. Publishers, , 1895) Accessed 15 Jan 2012 <http://history.rays-place.com/ny/boylston.htm>

Jefferson County. There are three Snyder heads of households in Ellisburgh: James, Isaac, and Henry[64]. Descendants of Henry refer to him as Henry Christopher. In addition, some of those descendants are found in Stephenson County near those of James in later census records. Although we cannot prove the exact relationships, it nevertheless seems logical to believe that James and Clarissa were settled surrounded with family.

*Moving together as community and family and being caring citizens were patterns in their lives.*

## WAR COMES TO THEIR NEIGHBORHOOD

Sackets Harbor was a village in Jefferson County about 20 miles north of Ellisburg, and was the "most important naval depot on the Great Lakes."[65] If the British gained control of this ship-building port, the Americans would lose much of their territory. Thus, for the men living in the area around Sackets Harbor, life became very unsettled. Because of the lack of "Regular" troops, American forces needed to rely on the Militia to defend the area.

On July 19, 1812, one month after the United States declared war, the British attacked Sackets Harbor and thought the battle would be easily won. As the battle began, calls went out to the countryside and farmers dropped everything, joining their militias ready to fight. The British were defeated. They controlled most of the area of the Great Lakes at this time, but did not have control of Sackets Harbor.

By the start of the 1813 fighting season, Captain Isaac Chauncey had been tasked with the goal of regaining

---

[64] see Ancestry.com
[65] "120 Years of Sackets Harbor", *Sandy Creek News*, 01 Jun 1932, 8.

They Did Their Duty

control of the entire Great Lakes region, and had taken his vessels near Fort George on the Ontario side. The Americans needed more ships, and used Sackets Harbor for their main shipbuilding port. The militia was used to protect the shipment of goods that would be used to construct the ships.

James Snyder was a part of this militia, enlisting for the first time officially on February 28, 1813, when 23 years of age, in the company of Captain Gad Ackley. He was five feet ten inches tall, with brown hair, blue eyes and a light complexion.[66]

Just as their predecessors who served in the Revolutionary War, these farmer soldiers learned to be "*ready at all times to go at call*" (my emphasis). Official enlistment and discharge records were not always exact. As Snyder's first attempt to apply for a pension was rejected due to insufficient official days of service, he tried to explain the expectations for militia service in his area:

> ...remained as a minute man in said militia during the whole time said war continued *ready at all times to go at call* [my emphasis] and when ordered out into the field of action would drop everything even his team and plow in the field to serve the country....[67]

Captain Ackley also tried to clarify this to the Commissioner of Pensions as he explained the amount of days he claimed to have served:

> ... according to his best recollection knowledge and belief he was personally and actually engaged in the service and behalf of the United States for at least one half of the time of the continuance of said war with Great Britain as above stated and otherwise in various services and capacities, that

---

[66] Pension file 21988.
[67] Pension file 21988, 16 Feb 1876 Affidavit.

he and his said company were ordered out and performed service for one, two or more days on various occasions other than those above named, that he has stated the dates and terms of his service as aforesaid according to his best recollection, that he was upon every occasion honorably discharged...from service but without any written discharge, that living in the immediate vicinity of Sackett's Harbor, Sandy Creek and other landing places upon Lake Ontario was the reason why he and his company and Regiment were so often called into service, and when not in actual service his company stood as minute men during the war, with government arms...[68]

This "off and on" military service is reflected in the service synopsis contained in the Snyder pension file. Unsigned, and written some time after 1881 (in that a book published in that year is referenced), the analyst notes that the battles at which Snyder claimed being present were not fought during times he was officially a member of the militia. Official records exist for enlistment periods from February 28, 1813 to March 18, 1813 and also from October 16, 1814 to November 14, 1814. However, in his affidavits Snyder also speaks of being present at the Battle of Horse Neck (Sackets Harbor) and the Battle of Sandy Creek. The first battle was in May of 1813 and the second May of 1814.

However, the author of the synopsis noted at this point that people in the militia here were called "minutemen" and that "organization on the Canadian frontier was to be in such efficient condition as to promptly turn out at every

---

[68] Pension file 12015, Ackley, Gad, War of 1812 Pension Files, Fold3.com, New York>A>Ackley>Ackley, Gad>11, accessed 15 Mar 2012.

alarm."[69] The notes tell of how General Brown, commander of the American forces at the second attack of Sackets Harbor in May of 1813, made a request for all the militia in the area of Sackets Harbor "which would include Snyder." The synopsis notes participation by the militia at Sandy Creek, and states "In both engagements the enemy were repulsed."

As the British prepared to attack Sackets Harbor on May 29, 1813, they landed on Horse Island, about a mile from Sackets Harbor. Horse Island was connected to the mainland with only shallow, fordable water at this point. We have no details of the battle from Snyder, but Captain Ackley gives an account as well as an explanation as to why the company did not remain in formation:

> Some time in the month of May A.D. 1813 he with several other officers was ordered to the quarters of General Jacob Brown at Brownsville for the purpose of consulting as to the plans of operation in said war, that it was agreed and so ordered by Gen. Brown that declarents Regiment and Company should march to Sacketts harbor immediately after hearing the reports of six 32 lb. guns at Sacketts Harbor and declarent was also ordered to march those of his company not having government guns to Sacketts harbor to be supplied with guns, that after remaining several days at Brownsville engaged in said business with Gen. Brown, declarent proceeded to collect those of his company without said guns and on the 28th day of said May 1813 while marching them to Sacketts Harbor for guns he heard said signal of six 32 lb. shots, that he immediately collected the remainder of his company and marched to

---

[69] Pension file 21988, Synopsis.

Sacketts Harbor on said 28th of May and on the 29th of said May he and his company were in the battle of Sacketts Harbor in which he had one man killed, that soon after the battle the declarent reported to Gen. Brown and requested that his company be discharged for the reason that he had no provisions, his men having had nothing to eat for twenty four hours, that General Brown declined discharging his company but gave us liberty to return to our homes and declarent and his company returned to their homes.[70]

No food for twenty-four hours, no provisions, and freedom to go home, but no official enlistment or discharge. This was life for the militia men of that area.

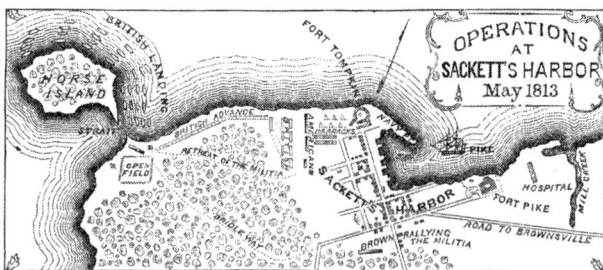

Exactly one year later, two ships being built at Sackets Harbor were waiting for their armament and rigging to be brought from New York to Sackets Harbor.[71] Nineteen flatboats had been loaded at Oswego, 50 miles south of Sackets Harbor, on Lake Ontario for the final leg of the journey. The British were eager to capture them to prevent the ships from being completed.

As the Americans prepared to make their way northward, they realized the British ships were blockading

---

[70] Ackley's text is given as written, with spelling and punctuation of the actual affidavit.

[71] Sackets Harbor is the present-day spelling, but in the early 1800s it was often presented as Sacketts Harbor or Sackett's Harbor.

the port of Oswego, so they tried to go under the cover of darkness at night as far as Stony Creek, about 12 miles south of Sackets Harbor. Realizing that they were not going to make it, they turned into Big Sandy Creek and made their way up the creek about a mile and a half. Some of the British followed, and one American flatboat got separated from the rest and captured by the British. The actual battle only lasted about ten to twenty minutes and the Americans won.[72]

Again the militia was there helping along with regular troops and some Oneida Indians. We find this recital of the events of the weeks just prior to and after the engagement directly from Captain Ackley's pension file:

> About the first of May A.D. 1814 about eight of ten British gunboats and barges entered the mouth of Sandy Creek Jefferson County and declarent immediately collected his said company and marched to said Creek to give them fight, but upon arriving there said British boats had gone out of the Creek into the Lake beyond the reach of our guns, that declarent then marched his company about two miles up said Creek where he and his company were encamped for three weeks, where the battle of Sandy Creek was fought May 29, 1814, that declarent and his company and a company of Riflemen composed the force on the part of the United States which fought said battle, and said gun boats and barges contained the British force, that declarent then being the Senior officer at Sandy Creek had the command in said

[72] Blaine Bettinger, "An Analysis of the Events Surrounding The Battle of Big Sandy and the Carrying of the Great Rope in 1814 and the Ensuing 185 Years" 1998-9. 20 May 2012.
<http://www.usgennet.org/usa/ny/county/jefferson/hounsfield/bettingerpaper.html>

battle, that the British loss in said battle was 27 killed, 35 wounded and 138 prisoners besides said ten boats loaded with arms and military stores, that declarent's company remained several days after said battle and were then discharged—that declarent was ordered to and was engaged as such officer for the term of two months and upwards in superintending the removal of said arms stores and other property taken from the British to Sacketts Harbor and in employing men and teams for that purpose and paying them off under direction of the proper Staff officers, that declarent was in said active service in said war after said British boats entered Sandy Creek and in the months of May June and July 1814 or thereabouts for the term of three months and was then honorably discharged from said service but received no written discharge;...[73]

The militia took care of transporting the shipment overland to Sackets Harbor, as related by Ackley. Hiram Downer, son of another company member echoed this in a declaration in Snyder's file:

...well remember seeing said James Snyder drawing heavy cannon with ox teams from Sandy Crick to Sacketts Harbor in the year A.D. 1813 and after the battle of Sandy Crick said James Snyder in company with my Father (Avery Downer) was ordered and sent on to Sacketts Harbor...[74]

Part of the rigging then stranded at Sandy Creek was an immense cable. Different measurements have been given of this rope, but it seems to have been about 20 inches in diameter, about 600 feet long, and weighed about four

---

[73] Ackley 12.
[74] Pension file 21988, Downer affidavit.

tons. Since it was too large to all fit onto one wagon, they loaded as much as possible onto the wagon, attached three pair of oxen to it, and then carried the rest on their shoulders.

> ...a crowd of men having made mats of plaited grass for their shoulders walked behind the cart in Indian file, staggering under the weight of the great rope that stretched like a long serpent back into the dim greenness of the woods.
>
> Finally men laid down their burden, sleeping that night in Ellis village. The next day the bearers of the strange burden made about 8 miles being fed and lodged most comfortably by the residents of the small settlements where they stopped. There were constantly a hundred men at the task working in relays. New volunteers were arriving and the old ones dropping out for most could not stand the strain for long.[75]

There is no complete list of the men who helped in the Great Cable Carry, but it is a testament to their spirit that whether they were officially "enlisted" or not, they served their country, and delivered the goods to the naval station so the ships could be completed.

## ON THE MOVE—AGAIN AND AGAIN

After the war, the Snyder family continued to grow, and at some point they moved south to a farm in Onondaga County, about one mile outside of Syracuse where they remained about 20 more years.

---

[75] Anna Jones Bartlett, "The Battle of Sandy Creek", *Watertown Standard*, 30 Jul 1926.

> *Moving and living together as extended family and supporting their country was central from the early 1830s to the end of the Civil War.*

In the early 1830s they moved farther west to La Porte, Indiana, where they remained about two years, and then to Ogle County, Illinois about 1836. Snyder gives a chronology of his residences in his pension file, and in an Ogle County history we find it confirmed with this statement: "The first settlers of this vicinity were David Hunter, Joseph Meyers and a Mr. Snyder, who settled here in 1836."[76] After about four years there, they settled in Rock Run Township, Stephenson County, Illinois. In the 1840's Snyder acquired several tracts of land and continued life as a farmer. The children married and bore children. Some died. Several sons and sons-in-law served in the Civil War along with at least two grandchildren, one of whom died at the Battle of Buzzard's Roost.[77]

At some point after the War of 1812, Snyder joined many militia members in submitting a claim for reimbursement for items used or depreciated during his time of service. We find a notation that he was awarded $36.00, and his address was Rock Run, Stephenson, Illinois. However, most of these claims were never paid.[78]

Well after the war Congress passed a series of acts whereby veterans could apply for a warrant to be issued bounty land. Upon receipt of the warrant number, they could request a land patent, and could keep the land or assign it to another. Though this was supposed to be a huge benefit for the old soldiers, land speculators became

---

[76] *The History of Ogle County, Illinois: Containing a History... Etc.* (Chicago: H.F. Kett & Co, 1878, Internet resource), 615.

[77] *The History of Jo Daviess County, Illinois: Containing a History... Etc.* (Chicago: H.F. Kett & Co, 1878, Internet resource), 681.

[78] New York Adjutant General's Office, *Index of Awards on Claims of the Soldiers of the War of 1812* (Albany, NY: n.p., 1860), 250.

They Did Their Duty

involved in the transactions, so the veterans received small amounts of money in actual payment for the land while the speculators made millions. Some suggested it would have been cheaper in the long run for the government to have paid the veterans directly.[79]

Each veteran usually received 160 acres. In June of 1856 Snyder assigned 40 acres of land in exchange for money. In January of 1858 he received another warrant, this time for 120 acres and assigned it in exchange for payment.[80]

> ***Doing their duty to the utmost in serving their country was carried on through the generations.***

With the Civil War being finished, and the family grown and spreading out, one would suppose that James and Clarissa might now have settled into their "golden years." From their marriage in 1811 in Rome, New York, through the years of the war and farming in Ellisburg (Jefferson County), then back down to Syracuse, on through La Porte, Indiana, to Ogle County and Stephenson County, Illinois, they had borne a total of 14 children and had many descendants. Examining the pages of the Stephenson County census through 1860, one can see the families close together.

### TROUBLES ON THE HORIZON

However, something was amiss, and on or about the 1st of June in 1869, James Snyder "willfully deserted Clara" and abandoned her. In September of 1873, she was granted an uncontested divorce, and the marriage was officially finished.[81]

---

[79] *Rock River Democrat*, 27 Mar 1855, 2.
[80] 21 Mar 2011 <http://www.glorecords.blm.gov>
[81] Pension File 34707, Snyder, James, War of 1812, National

What happened? After 62 years of marriage, how could it end in such a way? We may never know the truth, but there are some clues in the records that give us some possibilities.

Almira was his oldest daughter, married to Uriah Boyden. They were part of the early migration to Stephenson County, and farmed in Rock Run Township near her parents.

In examining the timeline of the disintegration of the Snyder marriage, the records reveal more clues. As he abandoned Clara (Clarissa) at the beginning of June in 1869, at the end of that month, son-in-law Uriah and daughter Almira recorded the fact that they had taken mortgages on Snyder's land in exchange for paying him $3,000.[82]

In the 1870 census, Clarissa is living with Uriah and Almira, while James Snyder cannot be found anywhere, even though another record claims he is still living in Stephenson County. His pension records claim he came to live in West Chicago by 1871, though his first affidavit applying for his pension was sworn in Stephenson County on March 10, 1871 (which would have been his 60th anniversary with Clarissa), where he claimed he was married and gave details of his marriage to Clara Downer on March 10, 1811 in Rome, New York.

Snyder did not appear in the Stephenson County Court the day the divorce decree was made. Clarissa was there with her lawyer and Uriah and Almira. She asked for "reasonable support", an immediate payment of one hundred dollars, the mortgage signed over to her, and a lien upon the lands for the payment of alimony. She also wanted her wayward husband to pay part of the court costs, and she would pay the balance. She received

Archives, Washington, D.C., 10 Jan 2011.
[82] *Freeport Journal*, Freeport, Illinois, Wednesday, July 14, 1869, 1.

everything she requested.[83] One might speculate that husband James had been paid to leave the area and not appear in court that day.

A biographical sketch for Uriah Boyden appears in a Stephenson County history, telling not only of his family, but also that of his wife. This book was printed in 1888, and the information for these biographical sketches was usually given by the family members. Here is what it says about Almira's family:

> Mrs. Boyden was born Jan. 18, 1811, and reared in Jefferson County, N. Y. She is the daughter of James and Clarissa (Downer) Snyder. Mr. and Mrs. S. lived on a farm and were natives of New York State. They subsequently lived and died at Turner Junction, Ill. The father had nearly attained one hundred years, when he died in September, 1886, his age then being ninety-eight. The mother died at the age of eighty-three, in 1887, in Rock City, this county. The father was a member of the Methodist Episcopal Church, the mother an Adventist.[84]

An analysis of the above paragraph shows several inconsistencies with other records, starting with the fact that James Snyder declares the marriage did not happen until March of 1811. Almira is either off by a year on her birth, perhaps being born in 1812, or James and Clara were married in 1810 (a distinct possibility).

Notice that there is absolutely no recognition of the divorce or any other marriage. The mother (Clara/Clarissa) is said to have died in 1887, but her tombstone and other pension records definitely say she died in 1877. If she were

---

[83] Pension File 34707.
[84] Portrait and Biographical Album of Stephenson County, Illinois: Containing.... (Chicago: Chapman Bros, 1888, Internet resource),193.

83 in 1887, her birth year would have been 1804, making her only seven years old at her marriage in 1811. Also, Clarissa never lived in Turner, though Mr. and Mrs. James Snyder lived there until their deaths.

The most glaring fact, though, is the absence of James Snyder's contribution as patriarch of several early families in the settling of Stephenson County. There is no biographical sketch of him and no recognition of his contributions to the county.

The last sentence towards the end of Uriah Boyden's biographical sketch can perhaps contain a clue of the interpersonal problems between the long-married man and wife and extending to part of the family: "The father was a member of the Methodist Episcopal Church, the mother an Adventist."

## ADVENTISTS

The Adventists had risen up in western New York in the 1830's under the leadership of William Miller. His followers were first called Millerites. They believed in the imminent return of Jesus to the world, and set a date in 1844. When the end of the world failed to occur, this became known as the "Great Disappointment."[85]

Various Adventist organizations continued, refining their beliefs, and some of their beliefs differed considerably from those of the Methodist Episcopal Church, including dietary and clothing restrictions. Adventists were known to be in Stephenson County at the time of the divorce, and some of the Snyder descendants were members of the First Day Adventist Church. Their differing beliefs could easily have divided the family.

---

[85] "The Rapture, Millerites, and the Great Disappointment". 20 June 2012. <http://historicaldigression.com/2011/05/20/the-rapture-millerites-and-the-great-disappointment/>

## PENSION POSSIBLE?

Even as Snyder was in the process of separating from his wife, the United States government was hearing more and more requests to give pensions to those who had served in the War of 1812, along with their widows. Many of those who had received the "Invalid Pensions" such as Daniel Wilson (see next chapter), had died, and there were few pensioners on the rolls.

Now Congress debated giving "Service Pensions" which would be given simply for serving a set number of days, and would have nothing to do with being injured or disabled. As they proposed qualifications for such pensions, debate ensued over keeping a "pauper clause" requiring "proof of Indigence on the part of applicants."[86] The Revolutionary War Pension Act of 1818 had such a clause, and because of it few veterans of that war ever even applied for a pension, and even fewer actually received them. Obtaining a pension from the government meant one did not have sufficient funds or family to care for oneself, becoming a matter of shame rather than honor.

Eventually Congress passed the Pension Act of 1871 for War of 1812 service. The final bill had no property qualification, and only a simple service qualification of 60 days, along with an honorable discharge. However, the applicant had to have been loyal to the Union during the Civil War, and swear an oath to support the Constitution.

The 1871 Pension Act also provided for surviving widows, providing they were married prior to the treaty of peace signed on December 24, 1814. All pensioners would receive eight dollars per month for the rest of their lives.

The government gravely underestimated the number of

---

[86] William H. Glasson, *History of Military Pension Legislation in the United States* (New York: Columbia University Press, 1900, Internet resource), 61.

people who would apply:

> By October 13, 1871, the Commissioner of Pensions reported that some 32,000 claims had been received under the law, and a new class of pensioners had been established. Of the claims received, about 25,000 were those of survivors and 7,000 those of widows.[87]

James Snyder applied for this pension on March 10, 1871, but the pension was rejected on July 6, saying he had only served 49 days.

Congress, pressured by their constituents, voted to sweeten the pensions. They passed a new law, the Pension Act of March 9, 1878, where the "widow restriction" was removed, allowing any widow married at any time to the veteran to apply. In addition, pensions would be allowed for only 14 days of service, no loyalty to the Union during the Civil War would need to be proven, and evidence of service and discharge could be established by means other than the official evidence—like affidavits from other people who were present at the incident.

This last part was crucial to many of the "minutemen" of the Jefferson County area, including James Snyder. This act also opened the floodgates for about 25,000 immediate new claims, most not by survivors or veterans of the war, but widows. Snyder reapplied, and on May 3, 1878 was admitted to the pension rolls at the rate of $8 per month, retroactive to the date of the act.

### A NEW LIFE AND A NEW WIFE

As James Snyder walked away from his wife Clara into a new life, he headed east on the railroad line to the fast-growing village of Turner. He found friends that he had known while in Rock Run, David and Sarah Springer. He

---

[87] *Ibid.*

They Did Their Duty

also became acquainted with a widow, Sarah Heslop.

Sarah Daniel was born in England, daughter of a carpenter, and in 1849 married Robert Heslop, a miner and later a railroad builder. They came almost immediately to Turner Junction, and Robert worked on the railroads until his death in September of 1871.[88]

On March 26, 1874, James Snyder and Sarah Daniel Heslop were married in Turner, and a marriage notice somehow made its way (with a few errors) to a New York City paper![89]

It appears that Snyder was not completely cut off from his family. In July of 1875 he sold three lots in Rock City to his son Perry for $500. Four years later Perry sold those lots for $200, less than half of what he paid his father.[90]

In 1881 a Freeport newspaper has this little notice: "Mr. Boyden was called quite suddenly last week to Turner's Junction, his father-in-law having met with an accident."[91] The newspaper did not state the nature of the injury.

In August of 1883, Snyder wrote to Johnsonville, Kansas asking his son Perry, who had settled there, to come see him as soon as possible, and that he, the father, would advance funds if necessary. Perry responded saying he would be there in a few days, and would accept money for the fare.[92]

James Snyder became known in Turner, including the fact that he was a soldier from the "Old War". Resident John West, who wanted to write a biographical sketch, wrote a letter to the Pension office in 1886 requesting

---

[88] Pension File 44278, Snyder, Sarah, War of 1812, National Archives, Washington, D.C., 10 Jan 2011.

[89] 22 Jun 2012 <http:fultonhistory.com> (Search "James Snyder" and "Turner, Ohio") *Stamford Mirror*, 1874, 10.

[90] *Freeport Daily Bulletin,* Freeport, Illinois, 30 Jul 1875, 4.

[91] *Freeport Journal*, Freeport, Illinois, 03 Aug 1881, 5.

[92] Pension File 21988, letter.

information on Snyder's age and service. "The old Gentleman is still living but too far gone for any information concerning his age."[93]

Truly he was "too far gone" because on September 2 of that same year, he died. Again, the wires picked up the story. In Syracuse, NY, the *Syracuse Standard* published this under the column "Gleanings":

> James Snyder, an elderly resident of Oneida and Herkimer counties, died at Turner, Ill., September 2, aged 98 years. He was born in Herkimer county in 1788, and was married in 1810 to Clara Downer, of Oriskany, by whom he had fourteen children, seven of whom are now living. In 1835 he removed from the neighborhood of Syracuse, by team, to Laporte, Ind., and in 1843 to Illinois.[94]

Notice that the above obituary gives his marriage in 1810 instead of 1811, the date he stated more than once in his pension file. This would fit with daughter Almira's birth being January of 1811. The date for arriving in Illinois is late, though, since he is listed in the census for Stephenson County, Illinois in 1840.

There was a more extensive obituary in the paper from the nearby town of Wheaton (IL), the *Illinoian*, and while particularly flowery, it does not have every detail the Syracuse paper had.

### James Snyder Dead—1788-1886

The distance between the two dates great as it may seem marks but the lifespan of James Snyder who died at his residence in Turner at one o'clock

---

[93] Pension File 44278, letter.
[94] "Gleanings," *Syracuse Standard*, Sep. 18, 1886, p. 1.

Thursday afternoon, September 2, aged 98. The century was well nigh rounded out a century more prolific in great events, since the time the child-like Nazarene, in peace and good will founded his mighty empire.

1788-1886, But two figures tell the tale yet measured by the importance of great events, we drift back, as it were, to the dark ages. Mr. Snyder was born in Herkimer county, New York. His early youth was passed in the counties of Oneida and Herkimer. About 1810 he removed to Ellisburgh, N.Y. at this time arose the war between England and the United States.

We find him along the first to respond to the call, and in 1813 enlisted at Ellisburgh, N.Y. in Capt. Gad Ackley's company of N.Y. Militia, Col. Sprague's regiment. He was in the battle of Horse Neck.

He again enlisted in the same regiment in 1814 and was present at the battles of Sacketts Harbor and Sandy Creek. The old gentleman was fond of recounting the struggles of his early days, his memory of the struggling times of 1813-14 and the embargo was fresher than on passing events.

He was one of the old line pioneers working his way into the wilderness of western New York where he made for himself a home for nearly a quarter of a century, from there he came to Michigan, Indiana, hence to the unbroken acres of Illinois, where in the near vicinity of Freeport at a time of life when a less sturdier man might look for quiet for his declining years he was to be found with ardor and elasticity of extended youth, forming anew and building afresh, a western home.

For some years he has been sensibly failing, yet his wonderful vitality carried him along, but the end cometh, and like the aged hemlock of his native state, with withered top, he lays himself down.

Mr. Snyder was twice married. He had fourteen children seven of whom survive him. He was a pensioner of 1814, a noble group, whose fading numbers may now be numerated upon the fingers of the hand.[95]

These are the surviving children referred to in the above obituary:

**Almira**—married to Uriah Boyden in Rock Run, Stephenson County, Illinois

**Lorenzo**—a farmer in Nora, Jo Daviess County, Illinois

**Jackson**—a farmer in Missouri

**Perry**—a farmer in Kansas

**Mary Jane**—married to Solon Beaman, living in Iowa (her sons founded the village of Beaman which still exists today)

**Cornelia**—married to Edward Webb, living in Nebraska

**Lucinda**—married to Omar Hazard, living in Iowa

By the end of 1886 Sarah started applying for a Widow's pension. We get more glimpses of Snyder's life in Turner from the affidavits contained in her file.

George and Martha Briggs were some of his first friends in town, and present at his marriage to Sarah. They had known Sarah and her first husband Robert Heslop for over 30 years and had lived as neighbors to them for most of the time.

Nelson Springer and his sister Kate swore that they had known Snyder for 20 years and were present at his death.

---

[95] *Wheaton Illinoian*, Sep. 10, 1886, p. 8.

They had known Sarah for 14 years, and also testified of the death of his first wife. These were children of David and Sarah Springer who had moved to Turner from Rock Run in Stephenson County. Nelson spent time as a locomotive engineer, and since Turner was the junction of so many railroads, it is not surprising that the family moved here.

Finally, in May of 1887 Sarah's pension was finally approved, and she lived with a young female companion until the end of 1896 before being interred by her husband in Oakwood Cemetery.

They Did Their Duty

# 4.
# Daniel Wilson

## "Doing his duty to the utmost of his ability"

One cannot think about Daniel Wilson without seeing the importance of consanguinity—blood relationships. His family sustained him emotionally and practically, and nurtured him not only in childhood, but throughout adulthood.

### THE WILSON HERITAGE

Born into the sixth generation of the Wilson family in America, Daniel descended from Henry Wilson who settled in Dedham, Massachusetts in the mid-1600s.[96] In viewing family records, it becomes obvious immediately that civic affairs, religious participation, land ownership, and education were important in their lives. Daniel's grandfather Michael as well as his father Michael both served in the Revolutionary War, along with many other relatives, many of whom led companies of men.

Daniel was the seventh child of Michael Wilson and his

---

[96] Ken Stevens, *Descendants of Henry Wilson of Dedham, Massachusetts*. Walpole, N.H. (P.O. Box 118, Walpole 03608: K. Stevens, 1996. Print. 67. Stevens gives the generations like this: Daniel[6], Michael[5], Michael[4], Henry[3], Michael[2], Henry[1]

wife Marcy, born January 12, 1796. The Wilsons lived in Rowe, Massachusetts (directly east of Albany, New York), and at some time between 1793 and 1800 moved to Orwell, Vermont (directly east of Ticonderoga, New York), where other family members had previously moved.[97] Michael's father died in 1804, and his father's brother Ebenezer took over the care of the estate and family.

In 1808 Uncle Ebenezer along with Daniel's paternal grandparents moved from Vermont to Genesee County, New York. Ebenezer was not a young man, having attained about 54 years. What drew them there when they were well settled in Vermont? Land, and more land, and perhaps the adventure of pioneering new territory. Their land would become Middlebury Township in 1812, and part of Wyoming County when it split from Genesee in 1841. It appears that Daniel and his family were a part of this migration.

> *Moving together as community and family and being caring citizens were patterns in their lives.*

On March 23, 1811, Uncle Ebenezer appeared in Richard Smith's Surrogate Court and was awarded guardianship of the "real and personal property"[98] of Daniel Wilson, who had turned fifteen on January 12. At that time period even if the mother was still alive, a minor child (usually until 21 for boys) needed a male guardian if there was any inheritance or property involved.[99] Women had no rights, so even though Marcy Wilson lived until 1829, he still needed a male guardian. Daniel also actually

---

[97] Stevens, 68.
[98] Genesee County, New York Probate Records, Letter of Administration, Vol. 1, Page 10.
[99] 15 Jun 2012 <http://www.answers.com/topic/child-custody-laws-in-the-united-states>

lived with Ebenezer's family for a time as his cousin Isaac, Ebenezer's son stated later in an affidavit telling of his early life to attest to the normalcy of his health:

> Isaac Wilson being duly sworn deposes and says that he has been intimately acquainted with Daniel Wilson of DuPage Co. Illinois from his boyhood almost uninterruptedly to the present time. That in his youthful days from about 13 years of age he resided with this deponent for several years (his Father being dead) And that the said Daniel in his youthful life and up to the time of his entering the service of the U.S. in the war of 1813-14 had enjoyed very uniform good health and was looked upon as possessing a sound and robust constitution.[100]

It is evident from the many affidavits contained in Wilson's legal records that he grew up surrounded by relatives.

In 1813 the War of 1812 began to involve New York in a more serious way. Commodore Perry had destroyed the British fleet on Lake Erie and the Americans had won a decisive victory on October 5, 1813 at the Battle of the Thames (or Battle of Moraviantown—see Daniel Benjamin's story). That had resulted in the death of the Shawnee Native Chief Tecumseh, and the destruction of the coalition that he had led. General William Harrison's troops were now being transferred to the east to try to gain Montreal. That left the Niagara region protected mainly with militia troops and a few regulars. By the end of 1813, though, the British began pushing back, and especially around Buffalo, the Americans began feeling very nervous.

In Batavia, a small village about 40 miles to the east of Buffalo, Daniel's Uncle Ira Wilson formed a Company of

---

[100] Pension file 24430, Wilson, Daniel, War of 1812, National Archives, Washington, D.C., 10 Jan 2011.

the New York Militia under Major Parmenio Adams' Battalion[101], under a Division commanded by Maj. Gen. Amos Hall. Daniel, not quite 18 years of age, volunteered for service about the 20th of December.[102]   Here is an account of what occurred in the next few days, written within the lifetimes of the participants:

## UNIVERSAL DESOLATION

On the 25th December, 1813, Gen. Hall had assembled at Black Rock and Buffalo 2,000 men. On the night of the 29th, the enemy were discovered approaching the American shore in great force. The militia were ordered to oppose their landing, but the main body fled on the approach of the enemy. Col. Blakesley's regiment, with other detached corps, amounting in the whole to about 600 men, formed in a line, and poured a destructive fire on the enemy as they approached the shore. They were, however, overpowered by numbers, and forced to retire. Gen. Hall retired with the remains of the dispersed militia to Eleven Mile creek, where he was able to collect only about 300 men to cover the flying inhabitants. The frontier presented one scene of universal desolation. "The miserable inhabitants who escaped the Indian tomahawk,

---

[101] In 1823, after Ira's brother Isaac Wilson had been declared winner of the U.S. Congressional Seat for their district, and had taken his seat in Congress, this Parmenio Adams, his opponent in the election, challenged his right to the seat in the 1st Session of the 18th Congress due to election irregularities. D.A. Hall and M S. C. Clarke. *Cases of Contested Elections in Congress: From the Year 1789 to 1834, Inclusive* (Washington: Printed by Gales and Seaton, 1834, Internet resource), 373-406.

[102] Pension file 24430

fled into the interior, without shelter or means of support, in the depth of winter, and subsisted on the charity of their friends."[103]

On the 30th, a detachment of the British crossed over near Black Rock. They were feebly opposed by the militia, who soon gave way, and were totally routed. Having set fire to Black Rock, the enemy advanced to Buffalo, which they laid in ashes, thus completing the desolation of the Niagara frontier.[104]

One might imagine the feelings of the farmers turned soldiers as they saw their dreams and generations of work in this land now going up in smoke. They probably wondered what sort of future their children and their offspring might have.

Daniel, whose 18th birthday was at that point less than three weeks ahead, describes the battle in this way in one of his affidavits contained in his later plea for a pension: "...that he was through that severe and disasterous [sic.] engagement *doing his duty to the utmost of his ability*" (my emphasis). After returning to Batavia, about the 10th day of March, 1814, he then reenlisted on May 1 in the Company of Capt. Abraham Matteson.

### REGULARS VS. MILITIA

At this point the Americans were especially feeling pressure to establish control of the Upper Great Lakes region and to finish the war because Napoleon was on the cusp of defeat in Europe.[105] That would then allow the

---

[103] John W. Barber and Henry Howe. *Historical Collections of the State of New York: Containing...State* (New York: S. Tuttle, 1842, Internet resource), 152.

[104] Barber & Howe 43.

[105] 15 Jun 2012, <http://almostchosenpeople.wordpress.com/2010/03/19/those-are-regulars-by-god/>

British to turn more attention to the war in America. They also were beginning to realize the need for and see the importance of trained "regular troops" versus mostly untrained militia volunteers. Because of this they rethought the way their troops were structured:

> While planning moved forward, Brown ordered two Camps of Instruction formed at Buffalo and Plattsburgh, NY. Leading the Buffalo camp, Scott worked tirelessly drilling and instilling discipline in his men. Using the 1791 Drill Manual from the French Revolutionary Army, he standardized orders and maneuvers as well as purged incompetent officers. In addition, Scott instructed his men in proper camp procedures, including sanitation, which reduced disease and sickness.[106]

By the beginning of July the regulars were ready to pursue the British across the Niagara River. General Scott had ordered regular blue uniforms for the men, but instead received gray jackets, generally worn by the volunteers. This actually worked to the advantage of the American side, because as the British saw the gray jackets, they confidently attacked, thinking they would easily rout them. Instead, the Americans led their men to victory on July 5, 1814, in what is now known as the Battle of Chippewa. Out of this battle came an unofficial motto, "Regulars, by God!", still used by the 22nd Infantry:

> The 22nd Infantry Regiment was part of General Winfield Scott's Brigade in 1814. Because of a shortage of blue cloth, the Brigade went into battle against the British at Chippewa, wearing jackets made of the only cloth available, in a "buff" or gray color. Because of their gray jackets, the British commander, Major General

[106] 21 Jun 2012 <http://militaryhistory.about.com/od/battleswars16011800/p/Chippewa.htm>

Phineas Rials, mistakenly supposed them to be local militia. However, as the 22nd and other units of the Brigade advanced through artillery and musket fire with unwavering military precision, General Rials corrected his mistake with the cry "Those are regulars, by God".[107]

"The next day, Brown was reinforced by a mixed force of militia and Iroquois under Brigadier General Peter Porter."[108] Captain Matteson's company, of which Daniel was a member, became part of this mixed force. According to Daniel's affidavit, they had served in Batavia (N.Y.) after enlisting at the beginning of May. On July 4, 1814 they marched to the Niagara Frontier and into Canada. Another company member, Marcus Spaulding, wrote of it in this way:

> July 4, 1814 marched with troops for Buffalo and the next day towards night arrived at the Cold Springs near Buffalo and on the 6th crossed Niagara River at Black Rock 2 or 3 miles below Buffalo into Canada and on that day this Deponent and the Troops went by a forced march to Chippewa Creek in Upper Canada and there joined General Peter B. Porters Army and arrived there about sun down.[109]

Again according to Daniel's affidavit, his company spent about two weeks at Queenston, Ontario, Canada, after the battle. They crossed the Niagara River to Lewiston, New York, were stationed at Five Mile

---

[107] 23 Jun 2012 <http://1-22infantry.org/history/historytitle.htm>
[108] *Ibid.*
[109] Pension file 2849, Spaulding, Marcus, War of 1812, National Archives, Washington, D.C., 21 Mar 2012.

Meadows, and then crossed back to Lewiston. Though the Americans were pleased with their victory at Chippewa, the troops were tired. Because of the physical exertions of that first week in July, Marcus Spaulding took sick, and was never again the same. Years later, he writes these lines in an affidavit as he attempts to claim an invalid pension: "Daniel Wilson Somewhere in Illinois was on duty with me at Chipewa the night I was taken sick the 7 or 8 of July 1814. If he could be found living he would swear to that."[110]

## BATTLE OF LUNDY'S LANE

The bloodiest, deadliest battle of the war and the destruction of Daniel's health were just ahead.

Beautiful to the senses was the morning of the 25th of July, 1814, on the banks of the Niagara River—a day memorable in the annals of the Republic. It was serene and sultry. Not a cloud appeared in the heavens, nor a flake of mist on the waters. The fatigued American army lay reposing upon the field of its late victory…when a courier came in haste with intelligence from Colonel Philetus Swift at Lewiston that the enemy[111]

You will probably recollect that Col. Philetus Swift with a part of the Pennsylvania Regiment of Volunteers, Major Matteson and Capt. M. R. Freeman with his company, were on the 21 July ordered across to Lewiston under the command of Col Swift. They left Lewiston in a hurry and lay at Schlosser [present-day Niagara, NY] at the time of the Battle of Lundy Lane 25 July.[112]

---

[110] *Ibid.*
[111] Lossing, 816.
[112] Pension file 24430.

Daniel was not resting that morning. The night before, July 24, he had been placed on overnight guard duty at 11 o'clock, just as he was ready to retire for the night. He had to serve without relief until morning two hours after sunrise, when he was finally relieved. Returning to camp, one mile away from his guard station, he was just getting ready to eat breakfast when the alarm was sounded, and the enemy attacked.

He retreated with his company four to five miles up the mountain, avoiding the road, running through the wood pursued by Indians fighting for the British. They then continued moving, covering several more miles.

> Having been driven to this extraordinary effort on a hot day the 25th July and up a heavy mountain, many of us found ourselves nearly melted, and badly exhausted, and then found no refreshment except drink; having lost all our provisions and Camp Equipage taken by the Enemy—and it was towards night on a circuitous route before reaching Schlosser having had neither Breakfast nor dinner, and too much exhausted to eat any Supper.[113]

There was still no time for rest. On the 26th he was sent back across the river (which took the effort of rowing in a river with strong current) with prisoners, and then to Batavia east. By the time he arrived home he was ill, and although he received permission to remain at home a few days he continued to decline. Within a week he was confined to bed and out of his head, deprived of reason for almost two more weeks. Because of his exertions, he would never again be a healthy able-bodied man.

---

[113] *Ibid.*

## HEAT STROKE

In today's world if one suffers heat stroke or heat exhaustion, we know one has to seek medical care.[114] As one dehydrates and the internal temperature rises, one stops sweating and the vital organs swell. If that body is not cooled down quickly enough, damage continues for days, weeks, and months "...the gut, lacking enough blood, gets leaky. Toxic substances excreted by gut bacteria seep out. That results in inflammation that can cause serious damage to other organs, especially the liver and kidneys."[115] Damage can last for years, and can affect any part of the body, including the brain. [116] Death also occurs in many cases, many times within the first three months.[117]

After recovering his reason, Daniel was very emaciated and enfeebled, but returned to duty at Fort Erie, working to the best of his ability until the end of his enlistment. Though both sides had claimed victory in the Battle of Lundy Lane in July, it was a turning point in the war.

In November of 1814 he marched again to Batavia where he along with other members of the company received his discharge paper. That paper later burned when his house burned, causing him many problems when trying to obtain a pension.

---

[114] "Heat stroke patients should be admitted to an intensive care unit for appropriate monitoring." Accessed 14 Feb 2012 <http://instructor.mstc.edu>

[115] 14 Feb 2012 <http://www.nytimes.com/2010/06/15/health/nutrition/15best.html?_r=1&ref=health>

[116] 14 Feb 2012 <http://www.livestrong.com/article/70749-residual-effects-heat-stroke/>

[117] 14 Feb 2012 <http://www.thehealthierlife.co.uk/natural-health-articles/healthy-living/heat-stroke-symptoms-00713.html>

The next years were very mixed as he came of age, married a woman named Betsey, and fathered four sons. His Wilson grandparents, his mother, and Uncle Ebenezer all died before 1830. Still living in Middlebury Township, Genesee County, New York, he suffered periodic bouts of great sickness, and was generally declining further in health.

Around 1834 his cousin Isaac, son of Uncle Ebenezer, decided to move further west with other siblings and assorted relatives to settle in Illinois, west of Chicago. Isaac Wilson had served as a New York state senator, was a representative in Congress[118] for a very short time, and was First Judge of Genesee County. In Illinois the Black Hawk Wars had just finished, and the land, black and fertile, was now available to settlement. Isaac Wilson was following the pattern of his father, moving to a new place in his mid-50's. Daniel was part of this group migration.

> *Moving together as community and family and being caring citizens were patterns in their lives.*

As the family arrived in Illinois, most chose land in Kane County. Daniel and family settled right next to the DuPage-Kane County border in Wheatland, a settlement no longer in existence south of present-day West Chicago. Daniel tried farming, and served as postmaster for the settlement.

Cousin Isaac, serving as postmaster in his Kane County village, soon became influential enough to propose a new name for the community where he had settled—Batavia.

In New York they had lived in the village of Middlebury, and had brought that name from Vermont. Batavia was the larger city near them, capital of the

---

[118] See footnote 101.

county, so perhaps they thought that name more appropriate than a third Middlebury.

> **Family was important to them, and they looked out for each other.**

By the mid 1840's as Daniel's health continued to decline, Cousin Isaac got involved, using the connections he had formed both in New York and Illinois and his knowledge of how the government works to help Daniel receive a pension.

### PENSION LAW AND QUEST FOR A PENSION

People who served their countries in war often did not receive a lot of monetary thanks from their nations. As the Revolutionary War commenced, the Continental Congress passed a weak pension law granting half pay for life for loss of limb or other serious incapacity. This was called an in-valid pension, meaning the person was NOT valid or able for military service. Later the word entered common parlance as a person handicapped in some way.[119] Unfortunately, this law was an unfunded mandate, with the states given the responsibility for funding it. Very few veterans ever received any invalid pensions or actual monetary compensation.

In 1818, the Service Pension Law was passed. This was for any person who had SERVED in the War for Independence (Revolutionary War), thus called service pensions. However, the huge limitation for this law was that the veteran would only receive a pension after proving he was indigent (the "pauper clause"), and of worthy character. Many never received anything.[120] Many never

---

[119] See definition of "invalid" on www.dictionary.com.
[120] 10 Apr 2012 <http://oldtimer.wordpress.com/military-tradition-history-veterans-abused-discarded/>

applied due to the stigma attached.

So, how could one receive an invalid pension, and did they give them to people who served in the War of 1812? Various acts were passed including the same provisions for invalid pensions for the new war as had been granted for the War of Independence veterans. In 1816 a full pension for private soldiers was set at eight dollars per month.

Daniel would need to prove that he indeed was disabled, was of worthy character and needed the money. In addition, the regulation demanded a sworn certificate from his Captain or other officer under whom he served proving the time and place of his having been wounded/disabled, and that the disabilities came while on active duty in the service of the United States.

In the National Archives of Washington, D.C., Daniel Wilson has a pension file, No. 24430. The first item in the folder is a pension file card. It says:

Pension No. 19020
Old War Inv.
Daniel Wilson of Capt. Freeman's Co., NY Militia
REJECTED

There is no date on this, and no hints of which materials in the file were submitted with this application and found lacking.

However, the entire file is filled with depositions and records that fill in details of what happened in that quest for a pension in those days and years. There are shadows of how the family was functioning to make sure Daniel was given relief.

On Nov. 5, 1845, in Kane County, Anson Root, a physician living in Elgin, Illinois just north a ways from Batavia, told how he lived in Middlebury, New York and had a commission in the capacity of a Surgeon of a battalion and afterwards a regiment in the New York Militia. He says he was a neighbor and intimately acquainted with Daniel.

He was called on to attend Daniel about the end of July 1814, and most of time since then had lived in the same town or in the vicinity with Daniel. He said he was well acquainted with Daniel and much of the time served as his family physician.

What he does NOT mention is that he was Daniel's cousin by marriage, married to Uncle Ebenezer's daughter Lucinda, sister of Isaac, and part of the family who moved from New York to Illinois.

Dr. Root swears that for a considerable portion of the time Daniel has had poor health "in consequence of his exposures and hardships as a soldier on the Niagara Frontier."[121]

On Nov 8, 1845, Daniel himself swore out a deposition detailing his petition.

## ANOTHER VERSION OF HIS DEBILITATING EXPERIENCE

On Dec. 10, 1845 a deposition of George W. Blodgett is recorded, given in Wyoming County (formerly Genesee), New York. He was a Sergeant in Daniel's company who joined Captain Matteson's Company about the same time. Soon after they all joined, Matteson was promoted to Major, and Moody R. Freeman took over as captain.

Blodgett essentially gives the same details of their marching the Niagara, down the river to Chippewa, going on to Queenston, then to Lewiston, down the river to Five Mile Meadows about two miles above Fort Niagara (then held by the British) and stationed there a few days. He then gives his version of what happened next:

> …on the evening of the 24th of July after dark we were all marched back to Lewiston a distance

---

[121] Pension File 24430.

of 5 miles and that on arriving at Lewiston said Daniel Wilson was detached and placed on guard where he remained on post without relief till the new guard was dispatched the next morning after Breakfast, and that almost a mile to his relief ... said Wilson proposed to this deponent to have some breakfast together which was agreed upon and this deponent went for the purchase of some molasses while said Wilson was baking some pancakes (although this deponent had eaten his breakfast before Wilson returned to Camp) and whilst said Wilson was preparing breakfast and before having eaten it the Alarm was given that the Enemy (British and Indians) were coming upon us in force and orders were immediately given to parade which was done said Wilson parading with the rest of the Co. before he had eaten breakfast and soon after a retreat was ordered but finding the Indians had flanked us and cut off our retreat by the way of the road Col. Swift Ordered Capt. Freeman who was acquainted with the Country to take the troops by a circuitous rout up the Mountain through the woods and into Schlosser and that the Indians followed us and kept up an occasional fire for a distance of several miles this deponent thinks as much as five. Although we retreated to utmost of our power and that we so continued to press on for a mile or two after the Indians fire had ceased where we got some drink many of us being nearly overcome with the heat it being a hot day the (25) July we the then took it more leisurely and arrived at Schlosser a little before night having lost all our provisions and equipage and taken by the enemy. and this deponent further saith that on the next day the Co. started for Batavia with prisoners taken at Bridgewater the evening before that so Wilson as this deponent was informed and truly believes was in a day or two after the said 25 of July taken sick and went home from Batavia and had a long and severe fit of sickness. And further that he did report himself to this deponent some time in the month of Oct. following although at that time in feeble health apparently this deponent being then at his residence on furlough and business for the Army and that said Wilson did go with him and assisted him in completing business and then went with him and joined his Company in Fort Erie the Regiment then being under the Command of Col. Hugh W. Dobbin and that said Wilson continued with and did duty according to his ability to the expiration of his time of service and then received an honorable discharge and further this deponent saith not.[122]

## COUSIN ISAAC USES HIS CONNECTIONS

Back in Batavia, on Jan. 7, 1846, Cousin Isaac wrote a letter to the Honorable John Wentworth enclosing Daniel's declaration, describing him as "a Cousin relative of mine whom you know as one of your constituency."[123] Wentworth had been elected to the House of Representatives in the United States Congress first in 1843, and represented northeastern Illinois.

Isaac mentions the fact that Jacob Wood, Jr. and Marcus Spaulding, men who also were in the same company as Daniel, were already on the pension roll. Towards the end of the letter, he asks Wentworth to give

---

[122] Pension File 24430.
[123] *Ibid.*

greetings to someone else in Congress, one with whom he has the "honor of being intimately acquainted."

Obtaining approval for the pension was not easy. The Treasury Department's Third Auditor's Office wrote a note to Wentworth dated Mar. 31, 1846, saying they had found Daniel's name appearing in Freeman's company, but the "rolls afford no evidence of his having sustained any injury while in the service."[124] It may have been at this point that the pension was "rejected" as recorded on that first card. The Wilsons did not give up.

On June 23, 1846, Isaac wrote Wentworth again, thanking him for his help, but this time telling him that the regulations of the Pension Office were impossible to comply with. Most of the officers were older than the young privates, many of them having served first in the Revolutionary War. All the officers involved were now dead, and none would be able to attest to the truth of how the injury was received.

Again he told Wentworth that he knew the rules had already been relaxed to grant pensions to several old soldiers of the same company, and that Jacob Wood, Jr. had an injury received in the same skirmish in the same manner as that of Daniel.

He now told him new depositions, one from a private and another from a Sergeant Blodget, were on the way to Wentworth by way of a Moulton Farnham through the Honorable Albert Smith, Representative from Batavia, New York. Isaac then asked Wentworth to go personally to the Pension Office to talk to them.

Continuing the perusal of these original papers in the pension file, Daniel gave another deposition in February 1846, followed by one by Cousin Ira Wilson, brother of Isaac, in March and one by James and Jacob Wood in

---

[124] *Ibid.*

April. All of them support the main story that the soldiers ran a long way, and Daniel was very exhausted at the end becoming sickly from that point on in life.

For whatever reason, it was at this point in May of 1846 that two more physician reports appeared. The first was from Dr. Daniel D. Waite, a physician in the Batavia (Illinois). Later, in 1859, he would move to Chicago and become the "mainstay" of the Chicago Medical Society until his death in 1869.[125]

The second physician's report was from Dr. Thompson Mead, Jr., son of General Thompson Mead from the War of 1812. Dr. Mead and family had come to Batavia from Chenango, New York, and his father and other family members had followed. The Wilsons and Meads surely were acquainted, and every connection pursued in this struggle to secure a pension. Both generations of Meads are buried in the Pioneer Cemetery located on the grounds of the Fermilab, Batavia, Illinois.

Both physicians' reports were very similar to that of Anson Root, and both agreed that Daniel's health had been ruined by the activity that took place in July of 1814.

By July 3, 1846, Rep. Wentworth wrote directly to J. Edwards, head of the Committee on Invalid Pensions about deciding Mr. Wilson case. The pressure was on.

### THE PENSION COMMISSION RECEIVES MORE CRUCIAL INFORMATION

In August a crucial piece of information arrived at the Pension Office. Moulton Farnham, a Wilson friend from Batavia, New York who also had family in that migration to Illinois, had gone to court and sworn a deposition. He said that on April 19, 1845, he spoke to Hugh Dobbin, an

---

[125] 22 Apr 2012 <http://libsysdigi.library.uiuc.edu/oca/Books200707/historyofmedicin00biog/historyofmedicin00biog_djvu.txt>

officer who had charge of the company at the end of Daniel Wilson's enlistment, when he was stationed in Fort Erie.

At that time Dobbin told him that General Peter B. Porter, Colonel Philetus Swift, Major Abraham Metteson, Major Sherman Lee, Captain Moody R. Freeman, Adjutant Ladowick Dobbins, Quarter Master A. Grun and Parmenio Adams, Paymaster, were all dead at this time. These were all the officers who could have given information as required by pension law on behalf of Daniel. In addition, Ira Wright, the Surgeon's Mate had moved to somewhere unknown to him and could not be found in order to testify.

At that time of service when Dobbin was in command, he said Wright had given him the number of the sick on the American side, but that he had never seen a list of their actual names. To his knowledge no such list had ever been written and thus, it would be impossible for Wilson to produce such a record to prove his injuries occurred while in active service.

In December of 1846 the case was referred to the Committee. Evidently it was not passed at that time. There is a note that in February, 1847 it was "carried over for want of time." [126] In March, 1847 it was again referred to the Committee, and in December of 1847 it was referred again. In January, 1848 it was again repressed.

Several undated notes from J. Wentworth are also in the folder, asking Edwards about what was happening with the pension. It is obvious that obtaining this invalid pension was not an easy task.

Finally, Wentworth took action in a different way. On February 13, 1849, he referred it to Congress. On March 3, 1849, the Congressional Record of the United States Congress records an Invalid Pension Act, Bill 780, in Vol.

---

[126] Pension File 24430.

2, Page 452-3. It tells the story of what happened to Daniel Wilson, and then awards him a pension by Act of Congress:

CHAPTER CLXXXVL—.

An Act for the Relief of Daniel Wilson.

Be it enacted by the Senate and house of Representatives of the United States of America in Congress assembled, That the Secretary of War be, and he is hereby, directed to place the name of Daniel Wilson, of the county of Kane, and the State of Illinois, on the roll of invalid pensions, and pay him a pension at the rate of eight dollars per month, from the first day of January, in the year of our Lord eighteen hundred and forty-seven, to continue during his natural life.

APPROVED, March 3, 1849[127]

Now Rep. Wentworth could finally write another letter to Edwards in June of 1849, head of that Committee on Invalid Pensions: "Please place Daniel Wilson, for whom a special pension law was passed at the last session, on the Illinois rolls at Springfield...."[128]

However, Isaac Wilson never knew that his cousin had finally received the pension. He passed away on October 25, 1848.

Daniel lived until July 23, 1863, dying in the middle of the Civil War. At least two of his four sons (Walter and Orsemus) served in that war, one becoming disabled in an eerily reminiscent repeat of heatstroke in a hot summertime battle.

> *Doing their duty to the utmost in serving their country was carried on through the generations.*

---

[127] Congressional Edition, Volume 528, United States Congress, U.S. Government Printing Office, 1849.

[128] Pension file 24430.

They Did Their Duty

Betsey lived with another son, Francis, until her death on July 17, 1873. Daniel and Betsey Wilson are buried side by side in Oakwood, in the same plot as their son Walter Sprague Wilson and family.

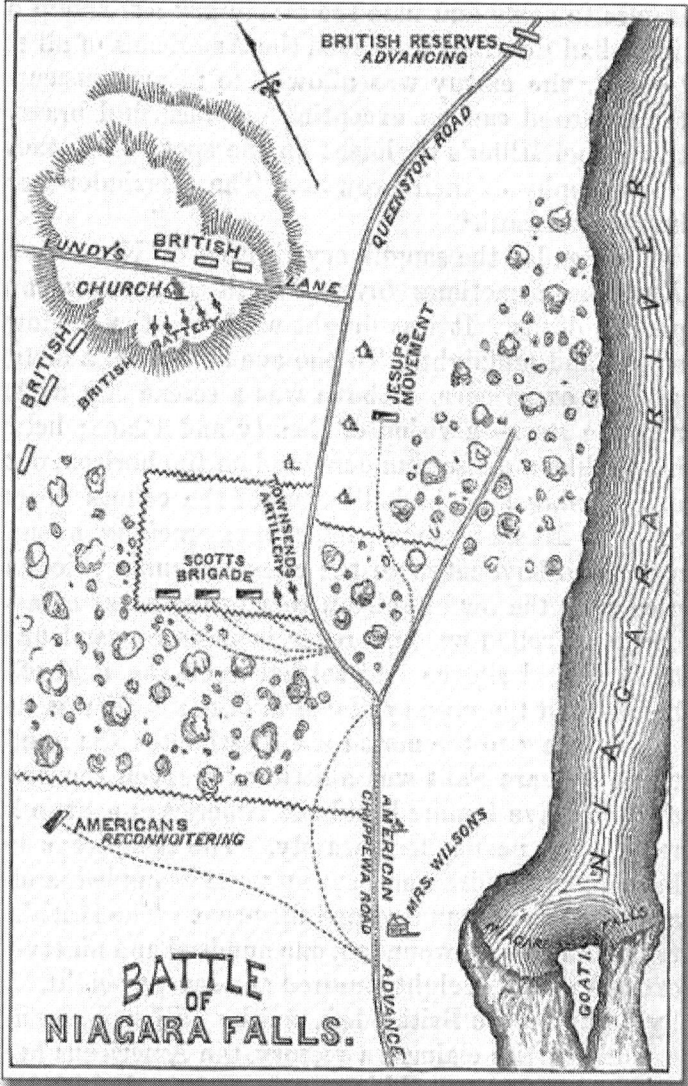

BATTLE OF NIAGARA FALLS.

They Did Their Duty

# 5.
# Daniel Wood

## "It becomes our duty, when required, to march to the defense of any section of the Union."

Daniel Wood came to DuPage County later in life, lived there only a few years, and died. Why would he move from his home place of Vermont where he had lived almost all his life and not remain there? Again, family played a crucial role, especially the family belonging to his wife, Sybil Holbrook.

### THE WOOD HERITAGE

Wood families came into the northern part of Franklin County, Vermont, just south of the Canadian border, between the Green Mountains on the east and Lake Champlain on the west in the 1700s. Daniel was born in Massachusetts on November 1, 1792, and evidently came to the Swanton, Vermont area at a very young age. He may have been the son of Daniel and Betsey (Potter) Wood, buried in Swanton in the Wood Cemetery. Details of several probable siblings have been gathered, but at this point little of his heritage is absolutely proven.

He was not, however, a new immigrant to the country. His wife was not newly arrived either, and, in fact, had a heritage that went directly to Governor Bradford, leader of the settlers on Plymouth Plantation for more than 30 years and author of a journal that is one of the prime records of our early northern history.[129]

A visit to the National Archives found proof of service in the company of a Capt. Elijah W. Wood (possibly his uncle) in the Vermont Militia under Col. Luther Dixon from September 15, 1813 for 3 months, serving 54 days and being discharged at Plattsburgh, N.Y. on November 18, 1813. A closer look at all the records, however, produced an stirring story of conflict between the governor of the state of Vermont, the militia recruits, and their burgeoning feeling of national pride as the War of 1812 continued to solidify the growing American nationality.

Between New York State and Vermont is Lake Champlain, a 125 mile long lake that is only 14 miles wide at the widest point. Towards the northwestern side of the lake is Plattsburgh, the county seat of Clinton County, New York, and the largest city on the lake. If the British could gain control of this city, they could control the entire northeastern section of the country.

Thus, militia companies composed of the citizenry of both states were raised up to protect the area:

> The plan of 1812 campaign was to garrison coast fortifications with local militia together with some Regulars while the main forces invaded Canada from Detroit and Niagara. The Plattsburg army was designed to protect the Vermont and New York frontiers, and therefore, nearly one-half its strength was recruited from Vermont.[130]

Not all Vermonters were happy about this conflict

---

[129] *Of Plymouth Plantation* by William Bradford is available in many libraries.

[130] Herbert T. Johnson, *State of Vermont, Roster of Soldiers in the War of 1812-14* (St. Albans, Vt: Messenger Press, 1933, Print), 6.

between the United States and British Canada. The lucrative trade with Canada, on their border, had been prohibited since the Embargo Act of 1807. The unintended consequence had caused economic hardship to some of the inhabitants of Franklin County. However, when the alarm was sounded, the townsmen were quick to respond.

## COMPELLED TO SERVE, BUT CHALLENGED BY GOVERNOR CHITTENDEN

In 1813 when Daniel joined Captain Wood's company the word "drafted" is used in several places in his files. There was no official military draft at the time, but he obviously felt compelled to serve, doing his duty.

The militia men crossed the lake and put themselves under the command of the regulars at Plattsburgh. Then, just before the end of their term, as they were thinking the British might attack, Governor Martin Chittenden of Vermont sent them a letter dated November 10, 1813.[131]

Governor Chittenden was the son of Thomas Chittenden, the first governor of Vermont. He was a member of the declining upper-class Federalist Party, and as such opposed to the war.

He was extremely upset that Vermont militia would be out of his jurisdiction under the command of a United States officer, and coming to the defense of a neighboring state that should have been entirely competent to take care of itself. Therefore, he ordered them to return to Vermont immediately.

Not only did he send the proclamation to Plattsburgh, but he also sent a man to the camp to distribute it. Lieutenant-Colonel Luther Dixon took exception to this, and "looked upon it as an attempt to incite insubordination in the camp, and ordered that the agent be flogged." [132]

---

[131] See Appendix C.

The officers then met and contrived a letter of response.[133]

In the letter they expressed their astonishment at his ordering them home and detailed their reasons for refusing "absolutely and positively" to obey. They did not believe their service to the country stopped at the border to their state, and that while they were in service to the country the governor had no power over them. They spoke a bit regarding the legality or illegality of his giving them such orders, and then broadened their remarks to a wider audience.

Perhaps realizing that the principles of this communication were of greater import than just to the governor of Vermont, they now addressed their remarks to the "world" speculating even on his motives for writing such a letter.

First, they considered it a "gross insult," saying that it seemed he thought them ignorant of their rights, and that he was doing it "to overwhelm our country with ruin and disgrace." They thought his motive was to embarrass the army, "to excite mutiny and sedition among the soldiers," and perhaps worse of all "to induce them to desert that they might forfeit the wages to which they are entitled for their patriotic services."

This letter of response was printed in newspapers all around the country for years thereafter, and has become historically important as being the only such letter written by officers to their commander.[134] If we view it in the historical setting, remembering that the Bill of Rights was ratified only 15 years earlier, we can see the pride in their being Americans with its attendant rights firmly demonstrated.

---

[132] 15 Jun 2012 <http://www.rootsweb.ancestry.com/~vermont/ChittendenUnderhill.html>

[133] *Ibid.*

[134] See Appendix C.

Nevertheless, as the threat of attack by the British waned, the Vermont militia crossed the lake and returned home.

## THE MILITIA HEARS THEIR FRIENDS' DISTRESS

In 1814 the threat became more immediate, and the militia gathered again. This time the governor let them go. The September 9th issue of the Burlington Gazette said this:

> We rejoice to find *our militia are turning out with a spirit that does honour to themselves and their country* [my emphasis]. There can be but one voice on this subject. Whatever we think of the war our country is dear to us, and we hope not to flee an enemy within our borders. The militia of Vermont have heard the voice of their friends in distress. They will protect their fire-sides and their altars. Great numbers are constantly passing through town.[135]

Elijah Wood's Company returned to Plattsburgh for eight days. Was Daniel with them? Maybe. Maybe not. It is unclear from the incomplete records. He himself never applied for a pension, and did not submit an affidavit providing details of his service in his bounty land applications. Thus, we have to rely only on the testimony of his wife or other company members. Sybil notes the service in 1813, for which she had direct proof of enlistment and discharge.

Captain Major Elijah Dee, one of the superior officers of their Regiment, left a record of his remembrances of that time period, written in 1825, as Guy Beebe, a disabled Vermont militia member, attempted to obtain an invalid pension:

---

[135] *Burlington Gazette*, 09 Sep 1814, p 3.

I, Elijah Dee... do testify and say that on the evening of the first Tuesday of September 1814 and understanding that the British troops were Marching against Plattsburgh, I together with a number of others my Townsmen set out for Plattsburgh when we arrived at or near the Sandbar...we organized into a company. I was chosen to take Command of the Company and we went as far as the Grand Isle that night and the next day in the afternoon arrived at Plattsburgh. After we arrived I repaired to General McCombs quarters and made verbal report of said Company. I informed him we had come to assist in defending the place and requested arms and ammunition to supply deficiencies among the volunteers which he readily granted and he also furnished us with provision from the public stores—before we had done drawing our provisions—a report came that the British had crossed the River at Pikes encampment and would attack the fort that night. It was understood to be the wish of Gen. McComb that the volunteers should fall back to the south and in case of an attack from the British troops to fall on their rear. We accordingly marched to Salmon River about 4 Miles and remained there until the 11th while we were here and after a considerable number of the Vermont volunteers had arrived we organized and formed into Regiment under the immediate command of General Strong. Capt Jesse Post took Command of the Company above named and I acted as Major of the newly formed Regiment. On the 11th of Sept aforesaid we received orders and marched to Pikes encampment with the rest of the

They Did Their Duty

Vermont troops and acted in concert until we returned to our homes.[136]

The Vermont militia, composed mainly of untrained but willing farmers could easily have been massacred by the British, but just before the British commander gave the orders to attack them, he received word that his forces had been defeated in the naval battle on the lake so he surrendered. Thus, the Vermont militia could return home as heroes.

Guy Beebe was never able to receive an invalid pension. Wounded in the hip and unable to work, he died in 1832, leaving no widow. However, it was noted several times in his file that he left 15 living children scattered over Vermont and New York.

### CONFLUENCE OF DATES

September 11, 1814, the Battle of Plattsburgh was won and reminds us of "9/11", a date that resonated anew 187 years later. Today in Plattsburgh on September 11, there is a poignant time of remembrance and re-enactment of the battle from 1814, coupled with a remembrance of September 11, 2001, and the enemy's attacks in the United States on that day.

Back in 1814, at the Battle of Plattsburgh, the Americans defeated a much larger British force in a naval battle that ended the northern portion of the war, and maintained United States hegemony. The British, fresh from their victory over Napoleon in Europe, were humiliated, and the Americans were jubilant. The Vermonters especially felt vindicated as seen in the words of a newspaper editorial written just five days after the battle:

---

[136] Pension file [Blank] Beebe, Guy, War of 1812 Pension Files, Fold3.com, Vermont>B>Beebe>Beebe,Guy

The militia of Vermont—the green mountain boys—have acquired and maintained the reputation of soldiers; they merit the applause of their country. They have gallantly volunteered to defend the soil of Americans, and the retreat of the British army is an evidence of the estimation in which they are held by our enemies…

We cannot but consider the events of this day as glorious to the Americans, and highly important to this section of the country. Considering the great disparity between the naval forces, and the dreadful odds at which Com. M'Donough fought, we are astonished at the result. Today when one visits Plattsburgh, one can see the pride they still have in what happened here in 1814.[137]

Governor Chittenden was not successful in being re-elected as governor at the next election.[138]

When, then, did Daniel and Sybil Wood move to Illinois? He lived in Swanton, Franklin, Vermont in the 1850 federal census with all his children, but in the 1860 federal census he is in Winfield Township, DuPage County, Illinois.

On April 22, 1853, he received 40 acres of bounty land in Clinton County, Illinois for his service in Capt. Post's Company in the Vermont Militia. In 1852 the government had passed legislation that allowed the veterans to resell their land directly to other people. Daniel Wood assigned this first bounty land to a Jesse Johnson, and probably received money for the sale.

On the 1st of October, 1855, Daniel Wood divested himself of all his remaining property in Swanton for the

[137] *Burlington Gazette*, 16 Sep 1814, 3.
[138] 20 Jun 2012, <http://freedomandunity.org/new_frontier/1812.html#>

sum of $4,650. He sold it to his neighbor, and probable brother, Orrin Wood.[139]

> ***Family was important to them, and they looked out for each other.***

In May of 1858, Wood's oldest son Haskel married New Englander Julia Childs in Kendall County, Illinois. He later became a physician and raised a family. Second daughter Jennie married Newton Hawks on December 15th, 1858 in DuPage County, and second son Henry married one week later on the 23rd in the same place. Henry's wife, Sara Stevens, came from Vermont before 1850, settling in Wayne, DuPage, Illinois. Her relatives intermarried with others in the Wood family over the generations.

Sybil Wood's sister Wealthea/Wealthy, husband Oliver Cromwell Wait, and their family were also in Wayne by the 1860 census, having removed their memberships from their church in Vermont in 1858. In addition, they had classified ads in the St. Albans newspaper for several months, trying to sell their farm from June to the end of 1856.[140]

Therefore, it appears that at some point in the mid to late 1850s the Woods and relatives moved to DuPage County.

> ***Doing their duty to the utmost in serving their country was carried on through the generations.***

The Civil War touched them as their sons and sons-in-law went to war. On January 29, 1863, Daniel and Sybil's third son, Hollis, died in a St. Louis hospital of wounds

---

[139] Tanya M. Remillard, Assistant Town Clerk, Town of Swanton, VT, "Daniel Wood Research," email to Cheryl Waterman, 22 May 2012.

[140] "Real Estate for Sale," *St. Albans Messenger*, accessed through genealogybank.com ($), various issues.

received in the Battle of Vicksburg the previous December 29. A small obituary appeared in the newspaper in St. Albans, Vermont—near where they had lived.

Henry Seymour Wood and wife Sarah moved from Illinois to Minnesota soon after the 1860 census, and Henry fought with the Minnesota 1$^{st}$ Light Artillery Battery for a short time in 1865. By 1910 he had moved back to Turner, named West Chicago by this time, and lived there until his death at age 101.

Meanwhile, back in Swanton, Vermont, Orrin Wood's son was named Seymour Henry Wood. He too served in the Civil War and years later, even after leaving Vermont and moving to Florida, he wrote many articles and gave many addresses on the "Ransom Guards of Franklin County" and how they served the Union.

October 31, 1864, Daniel Wood himself died, and was buried right near the front arch of the cemetery. His second batch of 120 acres bounty land was awarded to him that same year, and sold by son Henry on December 15 of 1864.

In May of 1878, after the Pension Act of 1878 had passed, allowing a service pension for a widow married after the war and for only 14 days of service, Sybil filed an application. Accompanying her in the court that day were her sister Wealthy Wait and another sister's (Alzada, married to Elias Wells Kellogg) nephew, William Kellogg Guild.

Wealthy testified that she had known Sybil for 68 years and was present at her marriage to Daniel Wood. William said he had known Sybil for 20 years. Sybil herself told of Daniel being a private in Captain Wood's Company of the Vermont Militia, and tells how they were married in Swanton by the Rev. Eben Dorman. They had only ever lived in two places—Swanton, Vermont and Turner, Illinois.

They Did Their Duty

A year later she had still not received the pension, and was told they needed more proof.

That June (1879) George Atcherson and J. W. Smith from Turner swore they were present at Daniel's death and there was testimony that they were of good moral character.

In July, Abigail Hungerford Kingman, daughter of sister Angeline Holbrook and Simeon Rice Hungerford, of Cass County, Michigan submitted an affidavit telling how at the age of seven years she remembered attending the wedding of Sybil and Daniel at her father's house.

Elias B. Hungerford and Sarah Hungerford Egbert submitted affidavits from Steuben County, New York the next month, also testifying to the fact that they were present at the wedding. All three of these people were children of Sybil's sisters. Nephew Elias is notable in that he invented and patented a glass window blind that led him to be more interested in glassmaking. Becoming convinced that Corning, New York, would be a perfect town for glassmaking, he persuaded investors to move to Corning and construct a glassmaking factory. Though his glass plant failed, glassmaking became a very important industry there and remains so today.

Finally, on December 9, 1879, Sybil L. Wood received her pension, retroactive to March 9, 1878 (the date of the Act). It was first for $8 a month, increasing later to $12 per month, until she died at the residence of her daughter Sarah, aged 79 years.

## PROOF OF LIFE IN TURNER

Because of living only a few years in Turner, it was difficult to find much information regarding his life in Illinois. To me, though, the best proof of Daniel Wood's life in West Chicago, is found in a document containing his signature dated December 25, 1858. This was just after two of his children had been married, and after he had only lived a short time in Illinois. It shows that his thoughts were not only on his family, but also his community and his future.

**Daniel Wood signed the formation papers as one of the first Directors of Oakwood Cemetery.**[141]

*Daniel's plot is just inside the entrance on the left.*
*The arch and fence are no longer present.*

---

[141] See footnote 4.

# 6.
# Enduring Symbols

## WHAT'S LEFT FROM THE WAR?

Today, when one asks average Americans what they know about the War of 1812, few people can give many details. In fact, this war is known sometimes as "The Forgotten War." However, there are lasting symbols from the war that have not retained that label.

People sometimes recognize the name of Admiral Commodore Perry and know that he had something to do with Lake Erie. The naval battles on our Great Lakes coupled with his command were vital for protecting our border in at least nine battles. He was called the "Hero of Lake Erie."

Some people also know of the Battle of New Orleans, the last land battle of the war which was fought in January of 1815, after the peace treaty had been signed, but not yet ratified. Major General Andrew Jackson, later President, was the leader of the American forces as the British attempted to wrest control of the area of Louisiana, recently purchased by the United States from France under Thomas Jefferson.

The frigate USS Constitution was one of the first six ships built for the United States navy, and is the oldest commissioned vessel still afloat. In the War of 1812 it proved that the United States could hold its own against the British navy, and earned the nickname "Old Ironsides" because of the way some attacks bounced off it as though it were coated with iron. Today it's a living history museum open to public tours.

In 1828, when the ship was in dry dock and the Navy was considering whether the ship should be refitted or scrapped, Boston poet Oliver Wendell Holmes, Sr. wrote a poem that immediately became so popular and effective that the ship was saved. Millions of school children in the next generations memorized that poem and many can still at least say the first verse:

*Ay, tear her tattered ensign down!*
*Long has it waved on high,*
*And many an eye has danced to see*
*That banner in the sky;*

The "banner in the sky" inspired what is probably the best known symbol of this war, our national anthem. Frances Scott Keyes was watching the Battle of Fort McHenry in Baltimore, Maryland, two days after the Battle of Plattsburgh on September 13, 1814. After a long night's battle, and it became clear to him that the "banner in the sky" still waved above and that the United States had won the victory, he penned the words of the poem "Defense of Fort McHenry" that fit a popular tune of the time. It officially became our national anthem in 1931 though it had been used by the Navy and most Americans for years prior to that time.

Washington, D.C., our newly constructed capital, was burned August of 1814, perhaps in retaliation for what the British considered wanton destruction by the American forces in Toronto, Canada. The President's residence was rebuilt just in time for James Monroe's Inauguration in 1817.

James Madison, known as the "Father of the Constitution" and the "last Founding Father" was president during the War of 1812, serving from 1809-1817. His very popular wife, Dolley Madison, was the first President's wife to be called "the First Lady of the Land." at her death. "According to the Smithsonian, the term 'first lady' was first used in 1849 by President Zachary Taylor in his eulogy of Dolley Madison. Before that, a variety of other terms were used over the nation's first 100 years."[142] Some of these terms were Lady, Presidentress, Mrs. Presidentress, and Lady Presidentress.

---

[142] Visit to James Madison Museum, Orange, Virginia, 16 Jun 2012.

They Did Their Duty

# 7.
# Common Themes and Lessons

We started this quest wondering how these four men came to be buried in Oakwood Cemetery in Turner, Illinois, and discovered the answer for each. We wondered what they did in the War of 1812 and learned more about that war. As we journeyed through their lives, we discovered some common themes:

### Americans

None of these men or their families were recent immigrants to this continent. They were all native born and some had been here for many generations. They identified themselves with this land.

### Age at time of war

Daniel Benjamin was the oldest, well into middle age, while the other three veterans were in the beginnings of their adult lives—17 to 23.

### Family (known number of children)

Daniel Benjamin    7
James Snyder       14
Daniel Wilson       4
Daniel Wood         7

## Military Service

All of the four veterans were volunteers, members of the state militias, and all served with the rank of private. None of them were professional soldiers or members of the regular army.

All had descendants who served in the Civil War.

## Mobility

All lived in more than one place during their lives and they moved in community, supporting each other in their families and among their friends.

Daniel Benjamin: New York, Pennsylvania, Ohio, Indiana, Illinois

James Snyder: New York, Indiana, Illinois

Daniel Wilson: Massachusetts, Vermont, New York, Illinois

Daniel Wood: Massachusetts, Vermont, Illinois

All had descendants who continued the movement westward, with almost all the movement motivated by opportunities for bettering their lives, especially in the availability of more land.

## Strength of Character

All exhibited incredible strength of character, accepting what life offered them, and persevering even in weakness of physical prowess. They were willing to uproot their lives to uphold their principles or to improve their possibilities even in their old age.

### LAST REFLECTIONS

We have no photos of any of the men. We have signatures of three, and do not know if Daniel Benjamin could read or write. There are still many unanswered questions regarding their military service and parts of their lives.

What we do have are models of character and perseverance. Over and over they saw themselves doing their duty, protecting their families and their land. They did not see themselves as heroes and were not lauded in their lives. They took what life threw at them, handled it the best they could with the support of their families and their community, and persevered.

As we learn from the past and strive to understand it, we can better appreciate our heritage and build on it, especially here in West Chicago. We will then be able to live our lives more fully as we seek to persevere and deal with what life throws at us today.

They Did Their Duty

# Appendix A:
# Benjamin Family
# Attack & Captivity

At this time the Indians were still quite restless and sought every opportunity to commit depredations upon frontiersmen. At the commencement of the Revolution they had become so troublesome in that part of the country that several of the Benjamin families and a few others, for mutual protection, had erected a block-house, and a small fort, where they had kept their families for some time, they knowing that a band of Indians were lurking around them, but while thus combined and protected the Indians did not dare to attack them, and the whites supposed that they had given the matter up and left. In this vain confidence, one pleasant Sunday morning, in the month of May, 1775, they sallied out to their respective cabins, to look at their gardens, etc. While thus divided, the Indians, who had been lying in ambush waiting for such an opportunity, rushed upon them and made prisoners of David Benjamin and his family, including his wife and six children, with some others. In this melee, Jonathan Benjamin and his family escaped with their lives by being on the opposite side of the river. David Benjamin, feeling provoked at the thought of being taken prisoner before he was disarmed, raised his rifle and shot and Indian, who fell off the fence and was supposed to be killed, for which, in a few minutes after, he was killed by an Indian with his tomahawk, at a moment when he was not suspecting any danger. This the chief expressed sorrow for when he found that his brother was not killed, but only had an arm broken. Our hero— David Benjamin, Jr.,--was the second eldest of this family of children taken prisoners, and who with their mother, were hurried away into a hopeless captivity, as soon as their houses were pillaged and burned. They were probably taken into Western New York, as David's children say their grandmother often told them that they were close to the Canada line, but not in Canada. This family remained prisoners for seven years, until the close of the war. One or two of the children having become so accustomed to Indian life, and having nearly lost their knowledge of the English language, refused to return to civilized life; among whom was David's only sister, who after she had married among the Indians and had two children, was recaptured by the whites near the Niagara Falls, but was so much dissatisfied with civilized life that she returned to the Indians, and was never again heard of by her friends. Among those who did return, were David and two brothers, and their mother, who lived to a great age, and died in Hocking county, Ohio. After their return they remained on the Susquehanna until David married, in the year 1795, when he, with his mother, and one or more brothers, moved to the Northwest Territory, near the mouth of the Muskingum river, here they remained about four years, when they moved about twenty miles from Marietta, probably in the northeast corner of Athens county. There they remained till May, 1805, or 1806, when they settled on the farm where Union Station now stands, and where David died, on the 17th day of July 1834, aged sixty-seven years, and where his wife died in 1835, supposed to be sixty-eight years old. David Benjamin was a frontiersman all his life, and so much of his youth having been spent among savages, he grew up without education, or much knowledge of the refinements of fashionable society, but he was a peaceable and a kindhearted citizen. He was cheerful, quite sociable, and very industrious. Although he often said he never could forgive the Indian race for the wrongs that he had suffered, still when a friendly Indian called at his door for bread, he never would turn him away till he supplied his wants. But when this was done, he would at once request him to leave. He seemed to fear that the remembrance of his wrongs would overcome his feelings of humanity, hence he would not suffer them to remain where they would be likely to tempt him, or excite his feelings of revenge. For some cause he entirely laid aside the use of a gun, and for many years kept none of his own.

## Meginness' Version

In the autumn of 1777 a band of hostile savages appeared on the Loyalsock and committed an atrocious outrage. Daniel Brown was among the earliest settlers in this part of the county. He had two daughters married to two brothers named Benjamin, and they lived near the cabin of their father-in-law. On the alarm of the approach of the Indians, the Benjamins, with their families, fled to the residence of Mr. Brown and made preparations to defend themselves. The Indians made an attack on the house but met with a stout resistance, which was kept up for some time. During the fight an Indian was killed by a shot from a gun in the hands of one of the Benjamins. This greatly enraged the assailants and finding they could not dislodge the besieged, they managed to set fire to the house. The flames made rapid headway and a horrible death stared the inmates in the face if they remained inside.

What was to be done? Remain inside and be consumed, or come forth to be, dispatched by the tomahawks of the savages? Either alternative was a fearful one. The Benjamins finally decided to come forth and trust themselves to the mercy of their foes. Brown refused, and remaining in the building with his wife and one, daughter, all three were consumed. When the Benjamins emerged from the door one of, them carried his youngest child in his arms. A burly savage brandished his, tomahawk and with a fiendish yell buried the glittering steel in the brain of Benjamin. As he fell his wife, who was by his side, shrieked and caught the child in her arms. His scalp was quickly torn from his head and exultingly shaken in her face.

The remainder of the survivors were seized and carried into captivity. This horrible tragedy occurred on what was long known as the Buckley farm, on Loyalsock.

The Benjamin families lived a few miles northeast of Williamsport. Three brothers and a small sister were taken prisoners. Their names were William, Nathan, and Ezekiel. The name of the one who was killed is not known, and the name of the sister has been lost. After a few years the captured boys were released and returned. The young sister grew up among the Indians, married, and had several children. Long after peace was made her brother William went after her and induced her to return. She remained here some time, but being always discontented and unhappy, she was permitted to return to her Indian comrades. What became of the wife of Benjamin, the meager accounts of the affair do not inform us, but it is probable that she was soon afterwards released.

This bloodthirsty attack, when the particulars became noised about, added fresh fuel to the flame of excitement and set the inhabitants wild with terror. That the Indians had entered into an alliance with the British to make an attack in the rear could be no longer doubted, and many families left the valley for better security. What could be done to stay the avenging hand of the savage? This was the grave and imperious question which stared every settler in the face. Must they abandon their improvements to the torch, remain, and be butchered or carried into captivity? The Supreme Executive Council had been appealed to in vain. Nothing, comparatively, was being done for their protection; but, instead, the constant cry was for men to reinforce the Continental army. Were ever pioneers in a worse predicament? Helpless to protect themselves; destitute of arms and ammunition; a few poorly clad and half-starved militia all that they could rely upon to stand between them and a powerful and wily foe, backed by the sympathy, encouragement, and gold of a strong nation. Such was the condition of affairs in the territory now composing Lycoming county in the closing months of 1777.

They Did Their Duty

# Appendix B: Governor Chittenden & the Vermont Militia

## PROCLAMATION CONCERNING THE MILITIA

### MARTIN CHITTENDEN, GOVERNOR OF VERMONT

10 November 1813

Whereas it appears, that the third brigade of the 3d division of militia of this state, has been ordered from our frontiers to the defence of a neighbouring state; and whereas it further appears, to the extreme regret of the captain general, that a part of the militia of said brigade have been placed under the command, and at the disposal of, an officer of the United States, out of the jurisdiction or control of the executive of this state, and have been actually marched to the defence of a sister state, fully competent to all the purposes of self-defence, whereby an extensive section of our own frontier is left, in a measure, unprotected, and the peaceable, good citizens thereof are put in great jeopardy, and exposed to the retaliatory incursions and ravages of an exasperated enemy; and whereas disturbances of a very serious nature are believed to exist, in consequence of a portion of the militia having been thus ordered out of the state:

Therefore-to the end that these great evils may be provided against, and as far as may be, prevented for the future.

Be it known, that such portion of the militia of said 3d division as may be now doing duty in the state of New York, or elsewhere, beyond the limits of this state, both officers and men, are hereby ordered and directed, by the captain general and commander in chief of the militia of the state of Vermont, forthwith to return to the respective places of their usual residence, within the territorial limits of said brigade, and there to hold themselves in constant readiness to act in obedience to the orders of brigadier general Jacob Davis, who is appointed, by the legislature of this state, to the command of said brigade.

And the said brigadier general Jacob Davis is hereby ordered and directed, forthwith, to see that the militia of his said brigade be completely armed and equipped, as the law directs, and held in constant readiness to march on the shortest notice, to the defence of the frontiers: and, in case of actual invasion, without further orders, to march with his said brigade, to act, either in co-operation with the troops of the United States, or separately, as circumstances may require, in repelling the enemy from our territory, and in protecting the good citizens of this state from the ravages of hostile incursions.

And in case of an event, so seriously to be deprecated, it is hoped and expected that every citizens, without distinction of party, will fly at once to the nearest post of danger, and that the only rallying word be-"our country."

Feeling, as the captain general does, the weight of responsibility which rests upon him, with regard to the constitutional duties of the militia, and the sacred rights of our citizens to protection from this great class of the community, so essentially necessary in all free countries: at a moment too, when they are so eminently exposed to the dangers of hostile incursions and domestic difficulties, he cannot conscientiously discharge the trust reposed in him by the voice of his fellow citizens, and by the constitutions of this state and the United States, without an unequivocal declaration, that, in his opinion, the military strength and resources of this state must be reserved for its own defence and protection, exclusively; excepting in cases provided for by the constitution of the United States; and then, under orders derived only from the commander in chief.

Given under my hand at Montpelier, this 10th day of November, in the year of our Lord 1813, and of the independence of the United States, the 38th.

Martin Chittenden

## RESPONSE TO GOVERNOR CHITTENDEN

1813

A most novel and extraordinary proclamation from your excellency, "ordering and directing such portion of the militia of the third brigade in the third division of the militia of Vermont, now doing duty in the state of New York, both officers and men, forthwith to return to the respective places of their usual residence," has just been communicated to the undersigned officers of said brigade. A measure so unexampled, requires that we should state to your excellency, the reasons which induce us absolutely and positively to refuse obedience to the order contained in your excellency's proclamation. With due deference to your excellency's opinion, we humbly conceive, that when we are ordered into the service of the United States, it becomes our duty, when required, to march to the defence of any section of the union. We are not of that class who believe that our duties, as citizens or soldiers, are circumscribed within the narrow limits of the town or state in which we reside; but that we are under a paramount obligation to our common country, to the great confederacy of the states. We further conceive, that while we are in actual service, your excellency's power over us, as governor of the state of Vermont, is suspended.

If it is true, as your excellency states, that "we are out of the jurisdiction or controul of the executive of Vermont," we would ask from whence your excellency derives the right, or presumes to exercise the power of ordering us to return from the service in which we are now engaged? If we were legally ordered into the service of the United States, your excellency must be sensible that you have no authority to order us out of that service. If we were illegally ordered into service, our continuance in it is either voluntary or compulsory. If voluntary, it gives no one a right to remonstrate or complain; if compulsory, we can appeal to the laws of our country for redress against those who illegally restrain us of our liberty. In either case, we cannot perceive the right your excellency has to interfere in the business. Viewing the subject in this light, we conceive it our duty to declare unequivocally to your excellency, that we shall not obey your excellency's order for returning; but shall continue in the service of our country, until we are legally and honourably discharged. An invitation or order to desert the standard of our country, will never be obeyed by us, although it proceeds from the governor and captain general of Vermont.

Perhaps it is proper, that we should content ourselves with merely giving your excellency the reasons which prevail upon us to disregard your proclamation; but we are impressed with the belief, that our duty to ourselves, to the soldiers under our command, and to the public, requires that we should expose to the world, the motives which produced, and the objects which were intended to be accomplished by such an extraordinary proclamation. We

They Did Their Duty

shall take the liberty to state to your excellency plainly, our sentiments on this subject. We consider your proclamation as a gross insult to the officers and soldiers in service, inasmuch as it implies that they are so ignorant of their rights, as to believe you have authority to command them in their present situation, or so abandoned as to follow your insidious advice. We cannot regard your proclamation in any other light, than as an unwarrantable stretch of executive authority, issued from the worst of motives, to effect the basest purposes. It is, in our opinion, a renewed instance of that spirit of disorganization and anarchy which is carried on by a faction, to overwhelm our country with ruin and disgrace. We cannot perceive what other object your excellency could have in view, than to embarrass the operations of the army, to excite mutiny and sedition among the soldiers, and to induce them to desert, that they might forfeit the wages to which they are entitled for their patriotic services.

We have, however, the satisfaction to inform your excellency, that although your proclamations have been distributed among the soldiers, by your agent delegated for that purpose, they have failed to produce the intended effect-and although it may appear incredible to your excellency, even soldiers have discernment sufficient to perceive, that the proclamation of a governor, when issued out of line of his duty, is a harmless, inoffensive and nugatory document-they regard it with mingled emotions of pity and contempt for its author, and as a striking monument of his folly.

Before we conclude, we feel ourselves, in justice to your excellency, bound to declare, that a knowledge of your excellency's character induces us to believe, that the folly and infamy of the proclamation to which your excellency has put your signature, is not wholly to be ascribed to your excellency, but chiefly to the evil advisers, with whom we believe your excellency is unhappily encompassed.

We are, with due respect, *Luther Dixon*, lieutenant colonel; *Elijah Dee*, junr. major; Josiah Grout, major; Charles Bennet, captain; Jesse Post, captain; *Elijah W. Wood*, captain; Elijah Birge, captain; Martin D. Follet, captain; Amasa Mansfield, captain; T. H. Campbell, lieutenant; G. O. Dixon, lieutenant; Francis Northway, lieutenant; Joshua Brush, lieutenant; Daniel Dodge, ensign; Sanford Gadcomb, captain; James Fullington, quarter master; Shepherd Beals, lieutenant; John Fasset, surgeon; Seth Clark, junr. surgeon's mate; Thomas Waterman, captain; Benjamin Follet, lieutenant; Hira Hill, surgeon's mate [*emphasis added for those mentioned in the Wood chapter text*].

# Index

2140684R00064

Printed in Great Britain
by Amazon.co.uk, Ltd.,
Marston Gate.